For the amazing John
Please keep inspiring
us all! We need that.

The Only Sustainable Edge

The Only Sustainable Edge

WHY BUSINESS STRATEGY
DEPENDS ON PRODUCTIVE
FRICTION AND DYNAMIC
SPECIALIZATION

John Hagel III
John Seely Brown

HARVARD BUSINESS SCHOOL PRESS
Boston, Massachusetts

Copyright 2005 John Hagel III and John Seely Brown
All rights reserved
Printed in the United States of America
09 08 07 06 05   5 4 3 2 1

Library of Congress Cataloging-in-Publication Data
Hagel, John.
    The only sustainable edge : why business strategy depends on productive
friction and dynamic specialization / John Hagel III and John Seely Brown.
        p. cm.
    Includes bibliographical references and index.
    ISBN 1-59139-720-0
    1. Strategic planning. 2. Business planning. 3. Business networks.
4. Strategic alliances (Business) 5. Technological innovations—Management.
6. Organizational learning. I. Brown, John Seely. II. Title.
    HD30.28.H323 2005
    658.4'012—dc22

                                                            2005003559

The paper used in this publication meets the minimum requirements of the
American National Standard for Information Sciences—Permanence of Paper
for Printed Library Materials, ANSI Z39.48-1992.

Jane Shattuck and Susan Haviland have contributed to this book, and to our lives, in more ways than we could possibly communicate—we dedicate this book to them.

Contents

Acknowledgments

This book represents the culmination of years of exploration for both of us. It would be folly for us to try to identify all the people who contributed to or influenced our perspectives over these many rich years of interaction, or even those we talked to specifically regarding this book. Instead, we will focus on acknowledging a smaller group who played a significant role in supporting the specific research we conducted for this book.

Victor Fung and William Fung, group chairman and group managing director, respectively, of Li & Fung, Ltd., provided us with some of the earliest views of the power of offshoring and loosely coupled process networks. Both Victor and William have been very generous with their time and very helpful in introducing us to others who are on the frontier of developing new ways of organizing business on a global scale.

We also want to single out a number of individuals affiliated with Crimson who aided us in developing the perspectives for this book. Crimson is the leading private equity firm focused on advising and investing in companies building offshore capabilities. John-Paul Ho, the managing director of Crimson, was particularly helpful and gave unstintingly of his time, contributing both perspectives and rich examples. His colleagues at Crimson—Fred Ayala, Cliff Chen, Rong Rong Liu, Ian Morton, and Drew Peck—were also very helpful in sharing their experience. Others introduced by Crimson who were very helpful include Derek Holley (president of eTelecare), Rick Zipf (CEO of Timogen), Sandy Ro, and Ajay Gandhi.

Mark Tucker, group finance director of HBOS, introduced us to a number of valuable contacts in India and China, including K. V. Kamath, managing director and CEO of ICICI Bank, and David Perrett, chief investment officer of PPM Asia. Prasad Ram, chief technology officer of Yahoo Software Development India, opened his Rolodex to us and introduced us to many key executives in Bangalore in addition to helping us to understand the broader significance of offshoring trends. Both Prasad and Ravi Venkatesan, chairman of Microsoft India, introduced us to the concept of "innovation blowback." Ravi also connected us with Rampraveen Swaminathan, vice president of the Power Generation Business at Cummins India Ltd., who provided us with a great example of innovation blowback in action. Nandan Nilekani, CEO, president, and managing director of Infosys, Vivek Paul, vice chairman and president of Wipro Technologies, and Kaushik Bhaumik, vice president of Business Technology Consulting for Cognizant Technology Solutions, were helpful in arranging meetings with their colleagues and providing us with great insight regarding the evolution of offshore software development and business process outsourcing. Jerry Wind, professor at the Wharton School, kindly invited us to attend a meeting of the International Academy of Management in Shanghai and assisted us in arranging some interviews in Shanghai.

A number of McKinsey & Company partners, including Jonathan Auerbach, Martin Hirt, Gordon Orr, Ranjit Pandit, Jayant Sinha, and Jonathan Woetzel, proved very helpful, both in terms of sharing their own insight and helping to connect us with executives active in the offshoring business. Lang Davison, an editor of the *McKinsey Quarterly*, continues to be a valued collaborator and gave us very good advice in sharpening many of our evolving perspectives on offshoring and the role of information technology in shaping business strategy.

Peter Volanakis, president of Corning, shared with us some excellent examples of productive friction in action, both related to the development of flat-panel display technology in Japan and of catalytic converters in the United States.

Peter Beck, managing director of Beck Group, patiently tutored us in the subtleties and complexities of the building industry, one of the earliest and best examples of process networks and productive friction in action. Peter also connected us with a number of his colleagues at Beck Group, as well as other participants in the building industry, to help deepen our understanding of the interactions that shape a building from concept to operation.

Marguerite Gong Hancock, associate director of the Stanford Project on Regions of Innovation and Entrepreneurship, introduced us to significant veins of academic research that were useful in shaping our own inquiry.

Paul Duguid has provided over the years critical insights into a practice-based theory of the firm. His ideas have served as a backdrop for many of our own notions in rethinking the purpose of the firm.

Kirsten Sandberg at Harvard Business School Press patiently worked with us and helped to focus both our thinking and our efforts to make this a more powerful book. Hollis Heimbouch at Harvard Business School Press also played an important role in making sure that we had the full support of our publisher in a very demanding project.

Carrie Howell continues to play an invaluable role as assistant and "command center" for John Hagel, helping to organize a chaotic life and keeping him focused on the things that really matter while still alert to events on the periphery. Without her help, including phone calls and e-mail messages at all hours of day or night, our trips to China and India in particular would have been far less productive.

We, of course, remain responsible for the product in the pages ahead. We continue to find it challenging and therefore exciting to explore the periphery and identify implications for those who must remain focused on core activities, whether in the realm of business strategy or public policy. Straddling the core and the periphery can be dangerous, especially when the periphery moves quickly while the core moves at a more determined pace. Patterns emerge and evolve but then, just as rapidly, morph into something quite different. We have chosen to focus on patterns that we believe will have lasting significance for all of us, whether in the core or the periphery. We will continue to report on how those patterns evolve. Interested readers should consult either the book Web site www.edgeperspectives.com or our Web sites www.johnhagel.com and www.johnseelybrown.com where we will strive to provide updates regarding our continuing research and findings.

The Only
Sustainable
Edge

Prologue

Collaborating to Get
Better Faster Everywhere

This book is not what it seems. Browsing through it, prospective readers might mistake it for a book that addresses the needs of business executives only, when it actually puzzles through problems quite common to policy makers, educators, and leaders of nongovernmental organizations. We urge these other readers, and indeed anyone interested in the forces reshaping our world in the twenty-first century, to read this book.

We have chosen to focus on business executives for one key reason. If business executives do not clearly understand the implications of these forces, the pace and scope of the changes discussed here will be significantly slower. As C. K. Prahalad cogently pointed out in another context, only business executives can ensure the scalability of new approaches. They must lead the charge for change. A compelling case must be made to reshape the business landscape—where and how value and profit get created—to create a scalable catalyst for broader institutional and policy changes.

Nevertheless, business executives cannot act in isolation. These changes are already reshaping our political, social, and educational institutions on a global scale, and these are just the beginning.

SHIFTING TO A DIFFERENT WORLDVIEW

We believe that a new opportunity and a new imperative—the acceleration of capability building—will shift our individual and collective mind-sets from a worldview that focuses on static, zero-sum relationships to one that emphasizes dynamic non-zero-sum relationships. As we adopt these different perspectives, we will find that most of our institutions today are fundamentally lacking.

Static, zero-sum worldviews generally arise when people focus on the allocation of existing resources. Existing resources have a fixed quantity, and with relatively modest exceptions, if one party acquires a resource, other parties are deprived of that resource. This worldview is a natural orientation of large, well-established players—they become more concerned with defending existing resources because they have a lot to lose on this front, compared with the opportunity to create even more resources. With its seventy-year focus on equilibrium states, the economics profession has reinforced this orientation. Equilibrium states are easier to model quantitatively, but such models simplify the world, including the key assumptions that capabilities and consumer preferences are a given.

If we recognize that capabilities are not a given, but can be quickly built, our worldview undergoes a fundamental shift. Now, we become less concerned with the distribution of rents and more focused on the creation of new rents. Relationships that were previously viewed as competitive become more complementary—we begin to realize that we need other specialized players if we wish to deepen our own capabilities more quickly. The new value we can create together moderates, even if it never entirely eliminates, the concerns about the distribution of proceeds. Physical and even intellectual property (at least in the sense of ideas that can be captured in patents or copyrights) becomes less central—although certainly not irrelevant—because this property is fixed in its capabilities. We begin to turn our attention more to the people we work with, because they hold the key to the acceleration of creatively building capability—and therefore the creation of new value. By discovering new uses for the physical and intellectual property we own, new capabilities in turn can help make this property even more valuable.

More generally, stocks of existing assets, including information and knowledge, diminish in value relative to flows of new ideas and experiences that can help accelerate our capability building. This is true for all institutions, not just business enterprises. In many cases, the institutional ability to accelerate capability building will depend as much on positioning in relevant flows as on the attributes of the institution itself. For this reason, this new worldview emphasizes the importance of the evolution of local ecosystems, global process networks, and communications and transportation infrastructures rather than focusing on institutions in isolation.

Comparative advantage also takes on a more dynamic quality. Traditionally, we viewed comparative advantage as the natural resources and labor costs that were relatively stable over time. As we begin to view comparative advantage in skills and practices, we realize that the advantage is far from fixed—it can shift rapidly as local ecosystems help accelerate capability building. Global patterns of production and trade will become much more dynamic.

WORKING WITH OTHERS TO
GET BETTER FASTER

The three elements that are required to accelerate capability building—dynamic specialization, connectivity, and leveraged capability building across institutional boundaries—are relevant not only to business enterprises, but to a broad array of political, social, and educational institutions. In this book, we suggest that these elements will ultimately force us to reevaluate the very rationale for the firm. In the same way, these elements will force us to reevaluate the rationale for most of our institutions.

In the commercial arena, the focus for value creation and value capture is shifting from product and financial markets to talent markets.

Institutions that can do the most effective job of accelerating the building of capability will create and capture value—the rest will inevitably fall by the wayside. We believe this will become the mandate—and organizing rationale—for all institutions, not just business enterprises.

Specialization has been an important engine of capability building and productivity gains from our earliest history. The emergence of agricultural societies almost twelve thousand years ago depended on specialization. The industrial revolution in the late eighteenth and early nineteenth centuries was made possible by even greater specialization. We are now seeing another wave of dynamic specialization building momentum and offering the prospect of productivity breakthroughs on a global scale. As one small example, health care institutions are realizing impressive productivity gains—measured as both quality and cost of care—as they become more specialized in dealing with certain types of illness.

Important advances in the technology infrastructure have made possible each wave of specialization. Broader institutions play a critical role in determining the pace of deployment and the effective use of this technology infrastructure, especially in the communications arena.

Specialization requires connectivity and effective methods of coordination. If enterprises cannot depend on other specialized entities to complement their own activities, they will avoid specialization themselves and suffer productivity penalties as a consequence. Connectivity requires far more than communications infrastructure. Trade, financial, and immigration policies all come together to determine the level and reliability of connectivity. Educational programs play a key role in facilitating the building of social and problem-solving skills as well as helping to establish shared meaning, even at the most basic level of language instruction. Social institutions and cultures shape openness to other beliefs and practices and therefore can enhance or undermine the potential for greater connectivity.

By connecting with other specialized institutions, we create an opportunity for leveraged capability building—getting better faster by working with others. To do this effectively, we will need to master the mechanism of productive friction. We'll discuss this mechanism in greater detail in chapter 5, but the term refers to the friction that can shape learning as people with different backgrounds and skill sets engage with each other on real problems if these people are provided with the right context. Productive friction is particularly valuable at boundaries because it exposes people to different ways of seeing problems and the potential solutions. These boundaries could be institutional boundaries, local ecosystem boundaries, or national boundaries. Again, nonbusiness institutions will play a significant role in shaping these boundaries, the opportunities to engage across these boundaries, and the tools available to enhance the productive potential of friction.

BOOTSTRAPPING AND THE RELATIVE RATE OF CAPABILITY BUILDING

These three elements—dynamic specialization, connectivity, and leveraged capability building—come together to help us get better faster. This book focuses on the acceleration of capability building within and across enterprises, but the opportunity and the imperative extend across all institutions. The convergence of these three elements creates a powerful bootstrapping dynamic—institutions, regions, and even countries can benefit from orchestrating these elements to move quickly from relatively limited capabilities to leading-edge capabilities, particularly in areas of specialization. Patterns of economic development around the world over the next several decades will be shaped increasingly by the relative convergence of these elements—and this in turn will depend on the shift in worldview to a more dynamic, non-zero-sum game.

As this convergence unfolds, policy makers and decision makers will need to avoid the trap of focusing narrowly on the absolute rate of capability building. Success in the global economy will hinge on an even more dynamic notion—the relative rate of capability building, particularly in comparable areas of specialization. If one area is building capability at a more rapid rate than comparable areas, it will overtake the other areas. Compounding effects alone will lead to this result, but acceleration effects are likely to further expand the gap over time. Capability building also tends to be path dependent, so that laggards have a difficult time trying to copy the process innovations of leaders. The only way to capture disproportionate rents in the long term will be to discover the unique mix of elements appropriate for any particular starting point and then actively manage these elements to attain and sustain superior relative rates of capability building.

THE GROWING POTENTIAL FOR
DISRUPTIVE INNOVATIONS

As we talk about accelerating capability building, readers might easily assume that we focus only on incremental, rather than breakthrough or disruptive, innovations. In fact, the convergence of the three elements that accelerate capability building will spur both kinds of innovation. In particular, as we discuss in chapter 3, large, emerging markets in China and India will spawn disruptive innovations in both products and processes, as companies race to serve the needs of growing middle classes that demand higher levels of performance at lower prices. These disruptive innovations will extend beyond commercial enterprises. Governments, health care institutions, and educational institutions are all seeking breakthroughs to serve their constituencies more effectively.

For example, Indian entrepreneurs are driving many of the initiatives to create more specialized health care providers so that larger portions of the population can get access to better-quality care at lower prices. The entrepreneurs are redesigning these institutions from the ground up to meet very aggressive performance targets. Cardiac care institutions like Narayana Hrudayalaya in Bangalore and the Escorts Heart Institute and Research Centre in New Delhi are demonstrating the value of specialization in medical care.

These disruptive innovations may emerge in offshore markets like China and India, where rising middle classes demand very different price points, but the innovations will not stop there. In time, they will migrate to more developed markets, winning share from more traditional players who complacently assume that what starts offshore stays offshore. This innovation blowback can happen very quickly. For example, the Indian health care entrepreneurs are already marketing their specialized services to patients in more-developed countries, encouraging these patients to travel to these facilities in India to get much greater value for their money. In a recent study, McKinsey & Company predicted that "medical tourism" could generate $2 billion in annual revenue in India by 2012.

In an epilogue to this book, we briefly explore some of the high-level policy implications of these changes in the commercial arena. For now, we urge nonbusiness readers to read ahead, even though the material might not explicitly address their concerns, because these changes will provide a context for institutional evolution and decision making around the world.

1

Beyond Margin Squeeze

Seeing Strategy Differently

W e live in challenging times, and our challenges are neither new nor temporary. Pressure has been mounting in business over the past fifty years and it shows no sign of abating. Consider these two long-term trends. First, between 1950 and 2003, profits of the nonfinancial corporate sector declined by two-thirds, from 18 percent to only 6 percent of the U.S. gross domestic product.[1] Second, the average time that a company spends on the Standard & Poor's 500 list has declined by 80 percent, from seventy-five years in the late 1930s to fifteen years in 2000.[2] Companies' departures tend to be sudden and severe, by acquisition or irreversible financial distress. So the challenge is not just profitability, but survival.

More than ever, we find ourselves walking a fine line between significant value creation and commensurate value destruction. One small misstep toward an irresistible opportunity can rapidly become an inescapable trap. So we search for a roadmap to guide our moves but fail to realize that our success depends as much on the lenses through which we view our options. Maps will help, but only if we see them with great perspicacity and from the right perspective.

In particular, we must regrind our lenses to monitor the periphery, that is, the edges, of our business. At these edges lie our richest opportunities for value creation and our strongest protection against value destruction. So what do we mean by *edge?* First, we mean the edge of the enterprise, where one company interfaces or interacts with another economic entity and where it currently generates marginal revenues rather than the core of its profits. Second, the edge refers to the boundaries of mature markets as well as industries, where they may overlap, collide, or converge. Third, we touch on geographic edges, especially those of such emerging economies as China and India, where consumers of all kinds crave Western goods and services that will ease their burdens and improve their lives. Finally, we refer to the edges between generations, where younger consumers and employees, shaped by pervasive information technology, are learning, consuming, and collaborating with each other and where baby boomers are preparing to retire or switch careers over the next decade. In this book, we argue that these edges will become the primary source of business innovation and therefore fertile ground for value creation.

Of course, managers cannot divert their attention completely from their core business and must learn to watch both the core and the edges simultaneously, without letting one distract them from the other. As bifocal as this sounds, the dynamic tension between the disparate demands of the core and the edge can lead to new insight and create new value. We hope to persuade you that the edge's importance is appreciating, yet most companies today still attend too little to the edge.

We also must adjust our lenses in another sense. Roadmaps can deceive users because they represent only a moment in time in a rapidly evolving business landscape. Yes, we recognize that the image of a volatile business landscape has become cliché, but most executives still dodge any attempt to look ahead and discern the distant contours. Instead, they typically grow ever more nearsighted, concentrating on near-term tactics since seeing over the next hill is too difficult.

We must recraft our lenses to compensate for this nearsightedness. Even if we cannot predict the future, we can certainly anticipate and, in some cases, even shape broad patterns of evolution. This foresight will help us choose wisely when we are allocating resources in the near term. Without illuminating, comprehending, and calibrating this background, we risk spreading our resources too thinly as we react to whatever crosses our paths along the way. Desperately diversifying our bets across an uncertain landscape, we may discover that our growing range of under-resourced experiments is tripping us up rather than moving us forward.

If we adjust our lenses accordingly, then we will begin to see something remarkable: the edges will reshape and eventually transform the core. We will begin to see how events at the edges of enterprise, the boundaries of our industries, and the large emerging economies will engulf the core, both challenging us and unearthing opportunities for innovation. In this context, the term *core* has two meanings. At one level, it refers to the inside of the enterprise—the core capabilities that determine our business success. At a global scale, the core refers to the developed economies of the United States, Western Europe, and Japan. On both levels, the patterns emerging on the edges will force us (and help us) to rethink and reconfigure our core activities.

As a result, companies must tap more effectively into the rapidly developing resources and opportunities emerging on the edge to amplify their own capabilities and initiate powerful new engines for innovation and growth. But, to do so, companies must undergo a fundamental transformation, deploying global business and technology architectures that exceed their own boundaries and span a growing number of companies across the globe. Those that aggressively reshape their businesses to exploit these opportunities will create significant value. Those that peer out through old lenses will endure increasing financial pressure and eventual widespread value destruction.

CONVERGING FORCES GENERATE
MARGIN SQUEEZE

Two forces have converged over decades to vex business executives. First, digital information technology began its inexorable march through the enterprise and through global communication networks. Second, public policy in diverse domains began shifting, intensifying competition on a global scale.

Rapid technology innovation in related spheres has enhanced the power and value of digital technology. Virtually everyone today knows of Moore's Law, whereby the number of chips that a microprocessor can hold will double every eighteen months. Even more accelerated innovation drives other domains of technology. A so-called fiber law and storage law work in parallel with Moore's Law to accelerate technology performance in related technologies. Fiber law anticipates the doubling of optical fiber performance every nine months. Storage law projects the doubling of the storage capacity of a single disk every twelve months.

In aggregate, these innovations have helped corporations extend their economic reach significantly. The innovations systematically enabled companies to reduce interaction costs—the costs required to locate resources (e.g., products from suppliers, inventories within a company, financial resources from investors, and skills of employees), obtain information about resources, negotiate access to resources, coordinate resources, and switch from one resource provider to another.

Interaction costs represent a substantial part of the cost of doing business. In developed economies like the United States and Europe, interaction costs represent as much as 70 percent of the total labor value-added costs, according to a detailed study prepared by McKinsey & Company. In developing economies like India, interaction costs are also significant, accounting for 40 percent of labor value-added costs.[3]

Of course, technology innovation does not automatically reduce interaction costs. To harness the full economic potential of information technology, management must change how it does business. Uncompromising companies like Wal-Mart, Charles Schwab, and McKesson became catalysts, innovating new business processes through the application of information technology, and forced others in the industry to adopt these innovations as well.

Technology innovations are opportunities not only for companies to create more value at less cost but also for customers, investors, and talent to increase their bargaining power relative to corporations by reducing their interaction costs as well. The net effect has intensified competition on all dimensions of business activity.

These innovations were accompanied by equally profound, long-term shifts in public policy—shifts that systematically eroded traditional structural barriers to competition, thereby enabling corporations to exploit the expanded reach obtainable through digital technology. These shifts also helped customers, investors, and talent increase their bargaining power, amplifying the parallel impact of digital technology.

More specifically, three broad public policy trends are helping to intensify the war for customers.[4] Deregulation is eroding structural barriers across industries, enabling companies to enter previously protected domains and offer new options for consumers. In the United States, competition is swelling in such industries as commercial banking, transportation, and electric utilities, and in countries around the world, governments have progressively dismantled the state monopolies and regulatory frameworks that had previously frustrated new entrants.

In tandem, trade liberalization is eroding tariff and regulatory barriers, enabling companies to compete on a truly global scale. Domestic companies that once crouched behind trade barriers are now facing competition from a growing range of foreign contenders. Customers who once had few choices now enjoy a much broader range of options in many markets, and so their bargaining power has increased. We see this trend most dramatically in Eastern Europe, where former members of the Communist bloc are shifting to more market-driven economies.

A third set of public policy trends involves the easing of restrictions on the formation, funding, and operation of commercial enterprise, thereby creating the conditions under which new companies could intensify competition within these markets and ultimately generate new competitors on a global level. Such market liberalization began reshaping the Chinese economy in the mid-1980s, swept through Eastern Europe and Russia beginning in 1989, and hit India with broad-based economic reforms in 1991.

These public policy trends—deregulation, trade liberalization, and market liberalization—have barely begun affecting some areas of the economy.[5] In others, they have already brought about significant change but hold the potential for greater effects over time.

Digital technology enhances the ability to exploit the resulting opportunities. Companies can support far-flung operations, setting up facilities in locations optimized for a particular business activity and expanding their marketing reach to new customer segments. Customers can access more information about more vendors, negotiate more effectively with still more vendors, and switch from one vendor to another whenever they find greater value.

At some level, all companies are customers of suppliers for their critical business needs. As such, they benefit from this shift in bargaining power. At another level, all companies have customers and will feel pressure from this shift in bargaining power. Consumers at the end of every business value chain ultimately benefit from these forces, but all other participants will have to deliver ever more value at ever lower cost.

Increasingly, we are seeing the emergence of *reverse markets*. That is, instead of vendors seeking to sell more goods and services to an even broader set of customers, customers are seeking the greatest value from a broader set of vendors at the relevant time and place. The reverse market increasingly reflects the dynamics set in motion by technology innovation and public policy shifts.[6]

These two forces—technology innovation and public policy shifts—have been rolling out since the middle of the twentieth century. Cyclical upturns and downturns have occurred, but the long-term secular trends have been consistent and sustained. Pressure is mounting, and managers should expect no relief.

CONFRONTING MARGIN SQUEEZE: THE EARLY RESPONSE

As margin squeeze mounted, companies responded in two broad ways since the 1980s. First, companies focused more on efficiency, relentlessly squeezing cost from operations wherever possible. Top executives launched a variety of business process reengineering programs, and total quality management programs and six sigma programs enlisted frontline workers, driving more efficiency into business processes from the top down and the bottom up. Simultaneously, corporations adopted a new generation of information technology (IT), namely, enterprise applications. These applications promised to standardize business processes across the enterprise and deliver substantial operating savings along the way.

Second, companies began to unbundle. The wave of conglomeration during the 1960s and early 1970s crested, then yielded to a series of divestitures and spin-offs designed to refocus companies on a much narrower core business. Mergers and acquisitions took off again in the 1980s and 1990s, but with a different business objective. Rather than diversification, they sought to build scale and scope economies within particular industries. Banks acquired banks. Media companies acquired other media. In many respects, these transactions simply delivered more operating savings to the bottom line. Companies also began to unbundle again. Outsourcing accelerated in the 1980s and 1990s, as companies continued to search for ways to squeeze costs and nonessential assets from their business.

Despite these efforts, executives express growing frustration with conventional strategies. More and more, we hear references to Lewis Carroll's *Through the Looking Glass:* "The Red Queen has to run faster and faster to keep still where she is."[7] Companies in general are failing to keep up. Traditional strategies no longer work. Managers must do something different or differently, and fast.

THE CONTOURS OF A
NEW BUSINESS STRATEGY

Companies are searching for a new way to cope with relentlessly intensifying competition. Managers understand that they must persist in generating operating savings, but mere savings no longer suffice: the savings are lost in competition and captured by customers. And in managing their steadily shrinking businesses, executives systematically destroy economic value for their shareholders and sacrifice jobs for their employees.

Analysts and consultants call on businesses to create more value through innovation, yet most companies have been optimized to produce greater efficiency, not greater innovation. As a result, any innovation-driven strategy will likely falter unless we fundamentally reframe our strategic thinking at three levels:

- Reconceive sources of strategic advantage

- Master new mechanisms to build advantage

- Adopt new approaches for developing strategy

Reconceive Sources of Strategic Advantage

Traditional structural sources of advantage—for example, geographic barriers, regulatory barriers, and economies of scale—have eroded. Squeezing savings from operations generally yields diminishing returns. In the search for new sources of advantage, two broad schools of strategy have emerged.

Integrating divergent strategic perspectives. In their influential book, *Competing for the Future,* Gary Hamel and C. K. Prahalad argued for basing a firm's business strategy on the core competencies of a firm.[8] We'll call this argument the core competency school of strategy, which built on a long-established tradition in academic literature. Known as the resource-based theory of the firm, it traces back to Edith Penrose's classic *The Theory of the Growth of the Firm.*[9] As presented by Hamel and Prahalad, this perspective remained very enterprise-centric: strategic advantage lay in clearly identifying and strengthening core competencies within the firm.

A second school of strategic thought—let's call it the leverage school of strategy—emerged a few years later with the publication of *Co-opetition,* by Adam M. Brandenburger and Barry J. Nalebuff, and *The Death of Competition,* by James F. Moore.[10] In these books, strategy focused less on capabilities within the firm and more on opportunities to achieve competitive leverage by mobilizing resources outside the firm. Using different labels—value nets and business ecosystems—these authors drew attention to the strategic advantages that managers can create by shaping and leveraging broader networks of resources beyond their individual enterprise.

Both these schools have vied for the attention of senior executives in the ensuing years. The relative success of the strategies has varied with the ebb and flow of broader business trends. During the exuberance of the late 1990s, the leverage school of strategy seemingly prevailed. A new senior executive position—the vice president of business development—emerged to focus on negotiating and managing relationships with strategic business partners. In the economic downturn starting in the year 2000, a back-to-basics zeitgeist ostensibly took hold. As executives turned inward, the core competency school of strategy resurged.[11]

Both these schools of strategy have merits. Companies can design strategies to fully exploit those internal capabilities that truly distinguish them in the marketplace, and companies can mobilize the resources of other companies to deliver greater value to their customers.

But, as presented, each of these strategies is incomplete. When customers demand more and control more, a company cannot rely solely on its own capabilities, no matter how distinct. Similarly, a company will struggle to mobilize outside resources unless it can offer exceptional capabilities in return. After all, the best enterprises receive so many proposals to collaborate that they will likely form partnerships only with whoever provides truly compelling, unique value. And so the real strategic power comes when a company integrates and extends these two schools of thought, amplifying the value of its distinctive internal capabilities by creatively and aggressively harnessing complementary capabilities from other companies.

Throughout this book, we use the term *capabilities* broadly to refer to the recurring mobilization of resources for the delivery of distinctive value in excess of cost. *Resources* refers broadly to both tangible resources (e.g., financial, human, and physical) and intangible resources (e.g., talent, intellectual property, networks, and brands).[12] These resources might reside within one's firm, or they might belong to other firms. *Mobilization* refers to both the practices and the processes required to create and deliver value with the relevant resources available.[13] Again, these practices and processes may reside within the firm, but they increasingly extend across other enterprises as well. Thus, resources, practices, and processes may extend well beyond an individual firm, and so the key strategic question for value creation becomes, Which firm can most effectively mobilize resources to deliver value for its customers?

We use the term *capability* rather than *competence* because the latter's common usage has tended to denote technology and production skills. For example, we could say that Dell has a distinctive capability in organizing pull-based production and logistics processes on a global scale. In contrast, Nike profits from its distinctive capability in creatively designing and marketing athletic apparel, especially footwear. Disney has a distinctive capability in creating multiple revenue streams from branded characters.

Taking a more dynamic view of capabilities. So far, we have discussed in relatively static terms capabilities as they exist today. As competition intensifies, managers who see their capabilities as static will find themselves rapidly outflanked by more aggressive competitors. The challenge is to accelerate and convert capability building into performance improvement as rapidly as possible—and across enterprises.[14] Remember that, according to the leverage school of strategy, competition increasingly hinges on the collective capabilities of business ecosystems or value nets, though we regard these terms as too broad for designing strategy. Consequently, we will later provide more precise descriptions of the various formations that businesses can take to collaborate and to rapidly enhance these collective capabilities.

In this context, integrating the two schools of strategy can help accelerate capability building across enterprises. The core-competencies school emphasizes the need for companies to develop a tight focus on areas of specialization and to be aggressive in seeking to deepen these over time. Companies with this mind-set are more likely to seek out ways to accelerate learning. The leverage school drives home the importance of looking outside the enterprise for complementary capabilities. This perspective helps ensure that companies expand their efforts to deepen skills beyond their own boundaries. Rather than looking inward, this perspective reminds us that a lot of the potential for capability building occurs when companies with very different specializations seek to collaborate around common business objectives.

In turn, by stressing capability *building,* we add a more dynamic aspect to the two schools of strategy. That is, distinct capabilities remain the basis of strategy but must rapidly evolve among collaborators to remain a source of strategic advantage. The competitive edge ultimately depends on a firm's institutional capacity to rapidly deepen its distinctive capabilities and to accelerate learning across enterprise boundaries, rather than simply mobilizing static resources.

Adding this dynamic capability element also helps shift economic analysis from a zero-sum equilibrium model to a positive-sum process model. So, rather than concentrating on dividing the economic pie, participants (whether employees within a single company or firms uniting around common business initiatives) can start focusing on opportunities to enlarge the pie overall. Of course, companies will still want to get their fair share, but distribution will matter less than getting opportunities to create more overall economic value. Moral hazard, cheating, shirking, holdup, holdbacks, principle-agent conflicts, and so forth, will remain very real issues in business; companies should still make institutional arrangements to mitigate these risks. We merely suggest that our more dynamic process view of capability building will put these risks into perspective.

By focusing on accelerating capability building as the source of strategic advantage, we underscore the importance of innovation, but we use the term more broadly than do most executives. Executives usually think in terms of product innovation, as in generating the next wave of products that will strengthen market position. But product-related change is only one part of the innovation challenge. Innovation must involve capabilities; while it can occur at the product and service level, it can also entail process innovation and even business model innovation, such as uniquely recombining resources, practices, and processes to generate new revenue streams. For example, Wal-Mart reinvented the retail business model by deploying a big-box retail format using a sophisticated logistics network so that it could deliver goods to rural areas at low prices.

Innovation can also vary in scope, ranging from reactive improvements to more fundamental breakthroughs. The approach to strategy outlined in chapter 7 explicitly seeks to moderate the scope of innovation. By emphasizing the acceleration of capability building, we are not restricting our focus to reactive or incremental innovations. Far from it. One of the biggest challenges that executives face is to know when and how to leap in capability innovation and when to move rapidly along a more incremental path. Innovation, as we broadly construe it, will reshape the very nature of the firm and relationships across firms, leading to a very different business landscape.

With the emphasis on capability building, we must look for areas that offer us the greatest potential for specialization and learning. For this reason, we must watch the edges of business activity for catalysts to capability building. As you will see, the edges of the business world, in the various dimensions described earlier, enhance the potential for capability building by bringing together many different specializations from many contexts.

Within this context, we propose that accelerated capability building is the most powerful source of strategic advantage in a global economy characterized by intensifying competition. In fact, accelerated capability building across boundaries is now the only sustainable edge, a proposition that we develop throughout this book. We build on the insights of the dynamic-capabilities school of business strategy by extending it especially across enterprise boundaries.[15] The relative pace of capability building matters most. Companies that embrace their edges will develop their own capabilities much faster than those that simply defend and extend their core operations and core markets.

Picture this as the natural extension of the open-innovation model used in product and technology innovation processes.[16] Open innovation rewards those who reach beyond their institutional boundaries and tap into specialized expertise distributed across many enterprises to strengthen product innovation. The open-innovation mind-set will help you think about accelerating capability building in general, not just about product innovation, but also about process innovation and business model innovation. It builds on the insight widely attributed to Bill Joy, one of the founders of Sun Microsystems, that "there are always more smart people outside your company than within it."[17] By embracing this insight, enterprises will start finding creative new ways to connect with a range of other companies to accelerate their own capability building.

Building this sustainable edge will require managers to focus on three broad strategic imperatives:

- *Dynamic specialization:* making difficult choices to focus on areas of world-class capability while shedding all other activities and then using the areas of world-class capability as a platform for aggressive growth

- *Connectivity and coordination:* learning how to access and mobilize the resources of other equally specialized companies to add even more value for customers

- *Leveraged capability building:* recognizing that the most effective way to accelerate capability building is collaborating closely with other specialized companies, pushing each other to become better faster

Again, various analysts have focused on individual elements of this strategic triad, but few have knitted the three into a new basis for strategic advantage. We believe that these three elements must converge on a global scale in a pragmatic, evolutionary way if a company is to create and capture value as competition intensifies. This book provides a different lens through which to interpret the evolution of strategic advantage and a pragmatic roadmap for magnifying that advantage by working with others to get better faster.

Rethinking the rationale of the firm. In his seminal essay, "The Nature of the Firm," Nobel Prize–winning economist Ronald Coase argued that firms exist to economize on market transactions.[18] All economic activity incurs transaction or interaction costs—the costs (and time) required to find resources, get relevant information about them, negotiate to gain access, monitor their use, and switch from one source to another if needs are not being met. Coase simply and powerfully argued that, under certain circumstances, firms provided a more efficient mechanism to access and use resources than do open-market transactions. In this view, efficiency was the primary motivation for the rise of firms. It certainly seemed to explain the rise of modern industrial firms as described in such classics as Alfred Chandler's *Strategy and Structure*.[19]

As information technology systematically reduces interaction costs both within the firm and across firms more broadly, the very reason for the firm's existence is changing. Perhaps we should reassess the continuing rationale for the firm, shifting it from efficiency considerations to capability building and systemic innovation.[20] This argument differs from (and relates somewhat to) that of the core-competencies school of strategy discussed earlier. That school contends that core competencies of the firm should serve as the basis for strategy. We suggest that accelerating capability building should serve as the basis for the firm itself. In *Knowledge, Institutions and Evolution in Economics,* Brian Loasby deftly argued for reconceiving the rationale for the firm in these terms, drawing attention back to the pioneering work of Alfred Marshall in *Principles of Economics.*[21]

From our dynamic perspective, the primary role of the firm should be to accelerate the knowledge and capability building of its members so that all can create even more value. This perspective broadens managerial attention from the tasks of allocating existing resources to the tasks of deepening knowledge and capability in an increasingly uncertain environment.

Master New Mechanisms to Build Capability Faster

Of course, executives may be skeptical. Why wouldn't companies want to build capability faster? But "wanting to" differs from "doing so," and that's why firms that actually accelerate their capability building will have such a powerful edge. Few do it well now, but new mechanisms are emerging to support companies in their efforts. Deploying these mechanisms will not be easy, because they collectively require profound institutional transformation, but the rewards will far outweigh the near-term pains of implementation.

Our book focuses on three mechanisms in particular:

- *Process outsourcing and offshoring:* the growing range of options to seek out specialized capabilities, wherever they reside, to support the core operating processes of the firm

- *Loose coupling of extended business processes:* using modular design and management techniques to mobilize distributed networks of specialized companies and create more flexible operating processes

- *Productive friction:* techniques to accelerate capability building by creating suitable settings for people with diverse and appropriate specializations to creatively resolve difficult business issues

We will define and discuss these mechanisms in more detail in the chapters ahead. Chapters 2 and 3 explore the co-evolution of process outsourcing and offshoring, highlighting their importance in expanding options for the dynamic specialization of the enterprise. Chapter 4 discusses the emergence of loose coupling as an alternative model for connecting and managing business processes that extend across multiple enterprises. Chapter 5 shows how productive friction can help address the challenge of building capability across multiple enterprises.

Emerging elements on the global business landscape will amplify the impact of these three mechanisms. Specialized local ecologies will enhance the attractiveness of process outsourcing and offshoring. Process networks will use loose coupling techniques to help companies access a broad array of specialized companies on a global scale for their business processes. Rapidly growing domestic markets in countries like China and India will serve as a catalyst for productive friction, forcing specialized companies to come together and develop innovative products, services, and processes to serve demanding customers in these markets.

Even with the benefit of these amplifiers, these mechanisms will be challenging to implement. In chapters 4 and 6 we discuss how performance fabrics help companies overcome these implementation challenges. Performance fabrics knit together business elements like shared meaning and reciprocal trust with technology elements like new IT architectures and software to help companies collaborate more effectively across enterprise boundaries. Performance fabrics become a key enabler, supporting the implementation of the three mechanisms and helping to effectively integrate them.

Executives can further reduce the implementation challenges by pursuing a pragmatic migration path to deploy these new mechanisms. Many companies are already embarked on the first wave of this migration path—shifting from a relentless focus on squeezing savings from the business to finding ways to more tightly specialize and to rely on other specialized companies through process outsourcing and offshoring. We will refer to this wave as the *specialization wave*.

In the second wave of the migration path, companies will begin to focus more actively on the challenge of coordinating process activities across a broad range of enterprises. They will learn to harness loose coupling techniques to create more scalable and flexible process networks and more effectively exploit the opportunities created by dynamic specialization. We will refer to this as the *connectivity wave*.

Finally, in the third wave of the migration path, companies will move from the coordination of existing resources to more sophisticated techniques that leverage capability building across large networks of businesses. Not only will their own performance improve more rapidly, but so will that of their partners. Companies that master the techniques of productive friction for learning with and from each other will become much more attractive as partners because they will deliver more value as part of the relationship—each party will come from the relationship with deeper capabilities and higher performance than before it entered the relationship. We will refer to this as the *capability building wave*.

We prefer to describe the migration path as waves, rather than stages. Stages suggest a strictly sequential movement, while waves offer a more realistic view of overlapping initiatives. In practice, most companies will see elements of all three waves in play at any point in time, but the critical mass of effort will likely evolve through the three waves.

These three broad waves will help deliver tangible business value at each stage of the migration path. Companies will move through these waves at a different pace. Many companies are already in the first wave, a few have developed the sophisticated orchestration techniques required in the second wave, and an even smaller number are starting to explore the opportunities created by the third wave. Each company must craft its own course through these three waves. There will be few, if any, shortcuts. Companies can certainly learn from the lessons of others ahead of them on the migration path, but since each path will be unique, every company must build its own capabilities in ways that are true to its own business practices. Given this path dependence, executives who start on this path sooner and who have a clearer view of the challenges and opportunities ahead are likely to reap significant rewards. As competition continues to intensify, those left behind are likely to destroy substantial economic value, because they remain locked into more conventional approaches for coping with the inevitable margin squeeze.

These three waves will help executives master the three mechanisms required to accelerate capability building—process outsourcing and offshoring, loose coupling, and productive friction—through incremental initiatives. Nevertheless, mastering these mechanisms will require considerable practice and process innovation, both within and across enterprises. The result will be a fundamental transformation of the enterprise.

Adopt New Processes for Developing Strategy

To move quickly along this migration path, companies must adopt new processes for developing strategy. As chapter 7 suggests, conventional approaches to strategy development are simply not adequate for coping with both the urgency and the uncertainty created by intensified competition. At the same time, we question whether much of the alternative thinking around emergent strategies provides enough focus for organizations as they seek to move quickly along the migration path just described. The pendulum may be swinging too far from directive, top-down strategy development in favor of approaches that emphasize large portfolios of experiments. Effective strategy development requires a much more balanced approach. As we will discuss in chapter 7, the productive friction created by a more balanced approach will help companies pursue breakthrough innovations as well as more modest, incremental innovations.

ANTICIPATING THE FUTURE

Imagine a company that works closely with a network of 7,500 business partners around the globe. It has about five thousand employees of its own and access to nearly one million more. It mobilizes this broader network to customize specific global supply networks for its customers. Given the specific product and service requirements of individual customers, this company assembles the right business partners to meet demanding cost, quality, and timing specifications. It can rapidly move specific business partners in and out of the supply networks to adapt to changing customer needs or market conditions.

This company also concentrates on building the capabilities of its business partners. It provides them with performance feedback and shares best practices from comparable companies around the world so that the entire network grows value for every participant.

Remarkably, this company generates over $5 billion in revenue— over $1 million per employee—and 30 to 50 percent return on equity. It has been growing both revenue and margins at double-digit rates over the past couple of decades, though it operates in a very low-growth industry characterized by razor-thin margins.

Not some high-tech fly-by-night, this company is approaching its hundredth anniversary. In fact, for many years, the company stagnated under increasing margin pressure with a very traditional business model. In the mid-1970s new management came in and reinvented the company. The process of reinvention continues today.

You've probably read about it already—Li & Fung, a company headquartered in Hong Kong. In many respects, it epitomizes many of the trends we described earlier. Li & Fung is

- active in the offshoring and outsourcing business, emphasizing its ability to orchestrate distinctive and specialized skills rather than simply delivering cost savings;

- highly specialized in its own enterprise but with sophisticated techniques to access and mobilize the resources of many other companies; and

- focused on the next wave of opportunity, promoting productive friction across its process network to improve the performance of its business partners and deliver even more value to its customers.

William Gibson, the noted science fiction author, has observed that "the future is already here, it is just unevenly distributed."[22] We can improve our strategy dramatically by monitoring the edges of our business world and studying companies like Li & Fung.

THE BOTTOM LINE

We have outlined a very different view of strategy for the firm. Most companies are pursuing some elements of this strategy already, but no company, at least to our knowledge, has all these elements in place today. To move successfully to this new strategy, senior management needs to develop a shared view of where it is today. Few companies have this shared view. Three quick diagnostics can help build this shared view within the senior executive team.

Migration path diagnostic. We outlined a three-wave migration path that all companies will follow to successfully implement this new strategy. We'll be developing a more detailed view of each wave of the migration path in the chapters ahead, but it would be useful to get the senior executive team to determine where the company is currently positioned across these three waves.

It is often revealing to look at this on two levels—first, in the enterprise's actual behavior over the past twelve months and, second, in its intended focus over the next twelve months. On the first level, identify the five most important operating initiatives undertaken—based on resource commitments—in the previous twelve months. Characterize the initiatives by their relative emphasis on the four elements discussed in this chapter—efficiency, specialization, coordination of third-party resources, and accelerating capability building across enterprises. Analyze implicit priorities across these four elements in two ways. Do a calendar review of senior executive team meetings over the previous twelve months, and determine how much time was spent discussing and reviewing the four elements of these operating initiatives. Next, roughly determine the resources committed to these four elements across these operating initiatives.

On the second level, perform a similar exercise across the five most significant operating initiatives to be launched over the next twelve months, again basing your assessment on resource commitments. Because management is now looking forward, it is usually harder to specify a broader range of operating initiatives. We thus recommend narrowing the focus from ten initiatives to the five most significant ones. For each of these five initiatives, characterize them by the relative emphasis on the four elements. Then roughly determine the resources committed to these four elements across these operating initiatives.

The results will often be a surprise, especially if compared with stated priorities. Senior management teams can use the results to reassess where they are allocating the resources of the enterprise, including the scarcest resource of all—their own time.

Outsourcing diagnostic. Senior management teams can use another quick diagnostic as a way to determine how aggressively they are exploiting outsourcing options and what the relative focus of their outsourcing initiatives has been.

To assess the impact of outsourcing in your company, first identify the amount spent on the outsourcing of activities over the previous twelve months. Categorize the various outsourcing relationships by their focus on three different forms of outsourcing—IT services, administrative processes, and core operating processes. Quantify the amount spent on outsourcing in each of these three forms. Determine how successful each of these three outsourcing forms has been in delivering anticipated performance. Estimate the relative amounts spent by key competitors on outsourcing in each of these three forms. If there are material differences, engage the senior management team in a discussion to try to explain these differences. Ask the senior executive team members to identify the next three categories of activities that they would choose to outsource if given a mandate to outsource more activities. What is preventing them today from outsourcing these activities, and what price is the company paying by keeping these activities?

Edge diagnostic. We emphasized the growing importance of the edge for business strategy—defined as the edge of the enterprise, the boundaries of industries, and the large, emerging economies that represent significant growth opportunities. Most companies invest very little effort in trying to understand events along these edges and in analyzing the implications of these events for the core business.

To give more attention to these events, engage the senior management team in defining the most relevant edges. Which five business partners are the most innovative in managing their own businesses? Which customers or customer segments are the leading edge in the use of your company's products or services? If significant new competitors were to enter your industry, what industries do they currently compete in? Which large, emerging economies represent the most significant source of growth for your industry?

For each of these edges, determine what efforts have been made over the previous twelve months to gain insight that might improve your business performance. Were these ad hoc efforts or part of a systematic process? What performance improvement has actually resulted from any of these efforts? How are you performing in these edges relative to your competitors? Has the senior management team directly sought to explore these edges? What could be done to strengthen the insight and performance improvement generated from these edges?

2

Offshoring

A Catalyst for Accelerated Capability Building

W e have just introduced the notion of accelerated capability building as the only sustainable edge. To understand how it has become such a powerful source of advantage, let's explore the dynamics and effects of offshoring in particular. Offshoring has attracted a lot of attention—and controversy—over the years. As with many other phenomena, we suspect that the near-term impact of offshoring has been significantly overestimated while the longer-term impact is equally significantly underestimated. The changes catalyzed by offshoring will play out over the long term, although we can already begin to see the broad outlines of the changes ahead. Offshoring pressures all companies to get better faster and simultaneously creates opportunities to work closely with other specialized companies to accelerate these efforts.[1]

OFFSHORING 101

Offshoring refers specifically to the movement of business activities to other countries to exploit cost or skill differentials. Offshoring may or may not pertain to moving operations closer to major markets, although distance from major markets indeed factors into the likelihood and the pace of a firm's offshoring efforts.

People often use the term *offshoring* interchangeably with *outsourcing*, although the two differ significantly. An offshore operation can be wholly owned by the parent company or it can be outsourced to a specialized service provider. Conversely, firms can outsource domestically—just look at the rise of specialized call centers located in North Dakota and New Mexico and that serve U.S. companies. Even though offshoring and outsourcing are distinct, they often become related operationally. Once a company has developed outsourcing skills, it will more likely consider moving its outsourcing relationships to companies offshore. Similarly, companies attracted to the specialized skills and cost advantages available offshore may find that they lack the scale or focus required to effectively access these capabilities with internal operations. So they will likely consider outsourcing to access these capabilities.

The Evolution of Outsourcing

Interest in offshoring has grown because of recent trends in outsourcing. Outsourcing swept over the corporate landscape in the 1980s and 1990s, as companies began to shed noncore business activities. The first wave, led by companies like Electronic Data Systems Corporation (EDS) and Computer Sciences Corporations (CSC), focused on outsourcing large-scale data centers and expanded into other IT operations like network management and storage management.

A second wave of outsourcing focused on administrative processes within the enterprise. Automated Data Processing (ADP) and other specialized service providers demonstrated to large companies that they could more efficiently handle the volume and complexity of payroll processing. Specialized service providers began to target other administrative processes within the firm. Human resource consulting firms like Hewitt Associates developed services to administer various human resource management processes on behalf of other companies. Exult (ultimately acquired by Hewitt Associates) developed a high-growth business focused entirely on outsourcing these human resource management processes. Large accounting firms like Arthur Andersen (through its consulting arm, now an independent entity operating as Accenture) and PricewaterhouseCoopers (now part of IBM Global Services) provided outsourcing services concentrating on finance and accounting processes within large enterprises.

A third wave of outsourcing began to target key operating processes within the firm. Companies like Celestica, Solectron, and Flextronics began to successfully outsource manufacturing operations for high-tech companies. Traditional delivery firms like United Parcel Service (UPS) and Federal Express expanded their operations to offer full-service outsourcing of logistics processes, including inventory management, procurement, and warehousing. Other specialized firms like Convergys (originally part of Cincinnati Bell) and Sykes targeted outsourced call center operations. Within particular industries like financial services, companies like State Street Bank and Trust Co. developed a broad range of outsourcing services focused on the specific back-office transaction processing needs of banks.

These waves of outsourcing overlap each other and illustrate a broad shift in the focus of outsourcing over time. In the first wave, executives were primarily looking for significant operating savings (both in operating expense and in asset leverage) by contracting with providers of relatively generic computing capacity. These outsourcing providers leveraged significant economies of scale to deliver savings to their customers. They generally did not need to understand their customer's business in any detail. The second wave of outsourcing required more specialized capability (e.g., keeping track of the myriad of rapidly changing payroll taxes for payroll processing), but still focused on relatively horizontal processes that operated similarly across companies from a variety of industries.

The third wave of outsourcing differs markedly. These outsourcers address the core operating processes of the firm. While operating savings still matter, they are not the only reason for outsourcing. In fact, in this third wave, the primary motivation shifts from accessing commodity capacity to accessing world-class capability. Companies are turning to these third-wave outsourcers because they need world-class capability in such activities, and they believe that they cannot achieve this capability on their own. By relying on specialized providers for certain core operating processes, companies can then focus on achieving world-class performance in the core operating processes that remain within their enterprise. In other words, specialization trumps savings as the motivation for outsourcing. In the process, companies are carving out core elements of their business and handing them off to third parties. As they grow comfortable with these outsourcing choices, executives are looking more broadly to find out where they can access world-class capabilities—and the search is increasingly taking them offshore.

The Evolution of Offshoring

Although the media often treat it as a recent phenomenon, the movement of U.S. businesses offshore has a long history. By the late 1960s and early 1970s, American textile companies had started to move significant production capacity from the United States into Mexico and various Asian countries. At the same time, U.S. electronics companies were relying on operations in countries like Mexico and Singapore for the labor-intensive stuffing of printed circuit boards. Texas Instruments opened its first R&D center in Bangalore, India, in 1985.

A variety of forces have converged since the 1990s to accelerate the movement toward the offshoring of key business activities in a growing range of industries. On the supply side, information technology has played a key role in making offshoring more feasible. In particular, the growth of communication bandwidth and the rapidly declining cost of this bandwidth on a global scale is key to facilitating offshoring. In addition, the declining cost of digital scanning and imaging technology has facilitated the transfer of document-based tasks like mortgage processing and image-based processes like X-ray interpretation to specialized offshore locations. In parallel, economic liberalization in areas like China, India, and Eastern Europe has helped foster investment in specialized offshore facilities. Finally, large pools of highly trained and underemployed college graduates, especially in engineering and other quantitative disciplines, have been growing in the same areas of the world. Relatively restrictive immigration policies in areas like the United States and Europe have encouraged companies to locate operations in these developing areas for better access to these skilled employees.

On the demand side, other forces have come together to increase interest in offshoring. As competition intensifies in developed economies, companies in these areas feel greater pressure to search more aggressively for ways to cut costs and to access distinctive skills. As some of the early movers in the offshoring field have reaped the benefits of these initiatives, pressure has mounted on other companies to follow suit. The economic downturn beginning in 2000 created even more urgency for companies to improve performance. Finally, the growth of a large middle class with more disposable income in countries like China and India has also increased interest in offshoring as a vehicle for more effectively addressing the needs of these large and high-growth economies.

Seeing Offshoring Differently

Unfortunately, most executives still view offshoring simply as a way to achieve near-term operating savings. As we will see, this view significantly underestimates the opportunities—and challenges—created by offshoring. Offshoring is a powerful way to rapidly build capabilities and reap the benefits of increased specialization. Rather than viewing offshoring solely as a form of wage arbitrage, think of it instead as a form of skill arbitrage supplemented by the opportunity to generate savings through more favorable wages. But even this underestimates the real significance of offshoring. Longer term, we anticipate that offshoring will become a powerful source of innovation in products and services. Initially, this innovation will be focused on serving the unique needs of demanding consumers in the high-growth emerging economies of China and India. Over time, though, we anticipate that this innovation will disrupt markets in the more developed economies as consumers in these areas realize that they too can get more value at lower cost. For this reason, we will focus our discussion on offshoring in this chapter on the countries of China and India.

OFFSHORING AS A WAY TO ACCELERATE CAPABILITY BUILDING

Offshoring provides a set of unique opportunities to accelerate capability building. For reasons we will discuss, replicating these approaches to capability building in more developed economies would be extremely difficult, if not impossible. This capability building delivers superior business performance today. Few companies would be prepared to move offshore some of their core operating processes like manufacturing, product design, and call center operation if the cost savings in any way jeopardized other dimensions of performance. In fact, sophisticated companies would not move an operation offshore unless they could also get superior performance along other dimensions. Discussing his call center operations, Michael Dell, the chairman of Dell Computer Corporation, observed that, "we will not offshore our call centers unless we can be convinced first that our customers would get better service than our own domestic call centers provide—any cost savings would be purely secondary."[2]

Superior Performance

What are some examples of superior performance from offshoring operations? Let's look at call center representatives. Based in the Philippines, eTelecare is one of the leading-edge call center operators in Asia. It has won numerous awards for the quality of its customer service, including the Best Outsourcer Award at International Call Center Management, the world's largest call center show, for three years in a row. The company serves a blue-chip array of U.S. clients, including a leading computer company and one of the most prominent financial services companies, both known for world-class customer service. eTelecare has reduced average handling time on inbound calls by 25 percent, relative to the client's call center or the previous outsourcer used by the client. It has done this while also delivering higher customer satisfaction. Ninety-nine percent of the client's customers indicated that they were satisfied or well satisfied, well above the initial target of 90 percent established by the client. In an outbound marketing campaign for one client, eTelecare exceeded the sales performance of the client's in-house facility after only one week. By the fourth week, the company was generating three times the weekly sales per hour and three times the client's in-house conversion rate.[3]

Performance levels are also high in offshore manufacturing operations. One large U.S. electronics manufacturer tripled manufacturing productivity (measured both in units per lines and in number of surface-mount technology components placed per unit of placement equipment) by moving operations from North America to mainland China. Cycle times were substantially reduced through process optimization, and defect rates came down as a result of a more rigorous focus on quality.[4]

Manufacturing costs can be further reduced through aggressive local sourcing initiatives that can yield 10 to 50 percent reductions in cost of goods sold, depending on the nature of the purchased goods, without sacrificing quality. For example, the purchased components for an industrial battery charger would cost about 50 percent less if sourced from local suppliers in China rather than the United States. The purchased components for mechanical landscaping equipment would cost about 40 percent less and the purchased components for industrial vehicles would cost 30 percent less than from comparable U.S. suppliers.[5] Of course, this assumes that capable local suppliers exist. Opportunities for such savings will likely be more restricted for more specialized or tailored components.

Moving product development offshore can also significantly improve performance beyond labor rate savings. In electronics hardware products, the time to market can be reduced by as much as 40 percent through offshore product development operations, especially when they are linked to offshore manufacturing operations.[6] Software development projects can shave 15 percent or better off the schedule, without a reduction in quality, by using experienced offshore teams in Asia.[7]

Accessing Distinctive Resources

Everyone knows about wage-rate differentials. Labor is less expensive in developing economies like China and India than in the United States, although the differential can vary significantly depending on the location, even within a specific country. But most discussions of wage-rate differentials tend to focus on low-skill job categories, comparing minimum-wage workers in the United States with entry-level factory workers in Asia. In fact, wage-rate differentials are also compelling in more skilled job categories. For example, the ratio of wage rates between the United States and mainland China for product engineers is about ten to one. The ratio for a software developer in the United States compared with one in India, meanwhile, is about twelve to one. This means that companies can access higher skills in these offshore locations at significant savings as well. Another way of looking at this is to compare the absolute wage premium to hire a college graduate versus a high school graduate. In the United States, the premium could run between $5 and $15 per hour, compared with a premium of $2 to $4 in the Philippines, so managers will more likely hire a college graduate in the Philippines.[8]

Distinctive skills. Of course, this discussion assumes that the required skills are available in offshore locations. In many areas, basic skills are not sufficient for the business need. For example, only a few countries in Asia could supply call center representatives to deal with American customers, because English-speaking skills are so limited.

On the other hand, many other skills are available in even larger numbers than exist in the United States, and the disparity is growing rapidly with each passing year. For example, China today graduates 350,000 engineers per year compared with 90,000 engineers graduating from U.S. engineering schools.[9] Most of the leading Indian IT outsourcing firms operate at level 5—the highest level of expertise—of the Capability Maturity Model (CMM), while most internal IT departments in the United States will likely operate at level 2 or 3.[10]

Many of these skills are quite distinctive. For example, in digital hardware technologies, product engineers in Greater China focus more on designing for manufacturability than do their typical U.S.

counterparts, who tend to be more concerned with pushing the envelope in features and product performance. In integrated circuit design, product engineers in Greater China have deep system-integration experience and a mind-set focused on integrating more functionality into a single chip using system-on-a-chip methodologies. Their U.S. counterparts, on the other hand, tend to focus more on designing the next leading-edge chip rather than better integrating existing functionality.[11]

China's skills are not just in the generic areas of design for manufacturability and integration expertise. Greater China is developing world-class design expertise in specific technology arenas. Some of the world's best designers of semiconductors for consumer electronics (e.g., chips for cellular telephones) are now based in Taiwan and mainland China.[12]

Companies in Greater China are also demonstrating leading-edge manufacturing process expertise in the production of key electronics components. As one illustration, Waffer in Taiwan has developed sophisticated thixomolding process technology to produce magnesium alloy casings for notebook computers with much higher yield rates of 90 to 95 percent, in contrast to industry standards of 70 to 80 percent.[13] Silitech, another company in Taiwan, has developed deep expertise in the sophisticated plastic and rubber composites now being deployed in the manufacture of advanced cellular handset keypads. Silitech started manufacturing handset keypads in 1988 and since then has rapidly evolved from basic rubber keypads to polycarbonate film and plastic and rubber composites. The company has also expanded its capabilities in the cost-effective design of keypads, requiring deep expertise in mechanical engineering, chemical process engineering, precision tooling for quality control, and a broad array of manufacturing processes.[14]

Cultural attributes. Beyond skills, distinctive cultural attributes help support accelerated capability building. John-Paul Ho, the managing director of Crimson, the leading private equity firm focused on advising and investing in the efforts of U.S. and other global companies to build out their offshore capabilities in China, suggests, "Cultural differences between the U.S. and Asia can undermine offshoring initiatives but, properly harnessed, they can deliver performance that simply would not be possible in the U.S."[15] Social networks and personal relationships play a significant role in Asian cultures and can often be used to bridge more formal functional and enterprise boundaries to ensure more effective knowledge sharing. For instance, Taiwanese companies very effectively compress product introduction lead times because of the personal relationships that facilitate close collaboration between system component companies and their suppliers.[16] These companies not only exchange staff, but also have often worked together in school or through prior work experience. In a more specific example of the importance of distinctive cultural attributes, many high-performance call center operations are choosing the Philippines as their offshore base because they value the traditional Filipino culture of hospitality and service.[17]

Distinctive Approaches to Accelerating Capability Building

Offshoring provides access to distinctive resources, but the real value comes from the opportunities to implement distinctive approaches to accelerating capability building—approaches simply not economically feasible in developed economies. By taking advantage of these opportunities, companies can improve the performance of their offshore operations more rapidly than would be possible if the operations remained in their domestic economies. Let's explore some of the key elements of these distinctive approaches to capability building.

Hiring more qualified people. To begin with, offshore operations can hire people who are significantly more educated and skilled for equivalent positions at considerably lower wages. By hiring better-qualified people at the outset, these operations increase the potential for performance improvement. In many cases, U.S.-based operations could not have hired equivalent skill sets at almost any price. Even if these more educated people could be hired in the United States, most managers would refrain from doing so, for fear that the people are "overqualified" and therefore would quickly leave. Many of these positions—call center operator and line assembly worker—are relatively low status in the United States. In contrast, in many offshore locations, these jobs are viewed as attractive opportunities to improve position. The workers are therefore more motivated to perform and, if given the right advancement opportunities, to stay. eTelecare, the Philippines call center company mentioned earlier, recruits top graduates from the region's leading universities, whereas equivalent graduates in the United States would simply not be willing to take on this kind of work. Competition for these jobs can be intense. As an illustration, eTelecare extends offers to only 2 percent of applicants and enjoys a 90 percent acceptance rate (compared with an average 50 percent acceptance rate in U.S. call centers).[18]

Lower manager-to-staff ratios. This quality-of-worker advantage is just the beginning, though. Companies exploit this higher potential for performance improvement by significantly shifting the ratio of managers to frontline staff. eTelecare, for example, maintains a team lead (frontline manager) to agent ratio of 1 to 8, compared with a ratio of 1 to 20 or even higher in the United States. Similar low ratios prevail at higher management levels as well in offshore locations because of the wage differentials at the management and agent levels. Derek Holley, president of eTelecare, observes that "we pursue many of the best practices of high-performing companies in the U.S., but the ability to cost-effectively support higher ratios of managers to staff gives us a significant advantage relative to our U.S. counterparts in terms of accelerating performance improvement. When you couple this with a higher caliber of agent at the start, we have an unbeatable advantage in building a high-performing organization."[19]

In contrast, high-performing organizations in the United States tend to strip out layers of middle management and to increase the operating span for the remaining managers, partly because of salary differentials. Highly paid middle managers need considerable leverage if the economics are to work, and so middle managers play administrative roles where they can maintain broad authority, rather than focus on more time-intensive skill building and process improvement activities.

Because of this heavier ratio of managers, eTelecare focuses its team leaders on skill building and process innovation. In measuring the performance of team leaders and other managers, eTelecare stresses their effectiveness in building capability and enhancing performance. For skill building, eTelecare invests heavily in formal training programs, but the team leaders combine apprenticeships, coaching, and mentorships to ensure that these training programs pay off.

For example, eTelecare agents who handle complex mutual fund advisory calls must take a sixteen-week training course leading to a test for NASD (National Association of Securities Dealers) series 7 broker certification. The eTelecare agents enjoy an average pass rate of 81 percent on these NASD tests (in recent test rounds, the pass rate has been 100 percent), whereas the average pass rate for the United States is 59 percent.

The heavier ratio of managers to staff allows for coaching that accelerates on-the-job performance improvement. For instance, eTelecare managers can provide more frequent and detailed performance reviews—at least one hour per rep per week for seasoned reps and more for newly hired reps. The result is that new reps can reach a 95 to 97 percent customer-experience rating within one month, at least 4 percent better than the performance in the in-house, U.S.-based call centers of their clients.

This focus on skill building contributes to rapid rates of advancement. High performers at eTelecare can rise from entry-level customer service agent to shift manager responsible for running a 150-person program in 2½ years. Training programs supplemented by apprenticeship and coaching at each level of management ensure continuing rapid development and advancement.

In addition to skill building, managers can spend more time searching for ways to improve service processes. At eTelecare, at least 10 percent of the team leader's time is spent on developing process improvements. The results are clearly evident when eTelecare takes over the call center operations of one of its clients. In one case, the client had experienced average handling times of about 8 minutes in its own operations. Within six months, eTelecare had reduced average handling times by more than 40 percent, to 4.5 minutes. This improvement came about through a series of refinements to the call handling process—for example, revising the order in which information was gathered and entered to minimize the impact on system performance and recommending changes to the screens to reduce the number of page changes required in most transactions.[20]

This approach of using lower ratios of managers to staff also applies in manufacturing operations. In a Chinese manufacturing facility, assembly line managers working closely with staff helped identify a novel way of using surface-mount technology placement equipment to reduce the lead time and cost of equipment setup. Identifying and grouping products with similar attributes led to significant reductions in throughput times and manufacturing cost.[21]

Drawing on the best of both cultures. Managing across two cultures can be challenging—it requires managers who can understand and respect the cultural needs of both parties. At the same time, it can create new opportunities to enhance performance by drawing on the best of both cultures.

Recall those call center operations in the Philippines. Filipino culture emphasizes hospitality and service, which helps Filipinos deliver superior customer service by quickly building rapport with customers and conveying true empathy. But Filipino culture tends to be very hierarchical—managers plan and workers execute. This cultural attribute hampers building a high-performance organization, since workers rarely take initiative or challenge managers constructively to avoid costly mistakes. To solve this problem, eTelecare fosters a nonhierarchical, performance-based culture and develops managers and leaders from within, rather than bringing them from the outside.[22]

Manufacturing operations in China are reaping the rewards of combining elements of American and Chinese approaches to process management. U.S. companies tend to be more systematic and structured in their manufacturing processes, ensuring consistency even with turnover in people. This approach, though, lacks flexibility. Chinese managers, on the other hand, tend to prefer looser job descriptions, permitting more flexible allocation of work among available people based on relevant skill sets. By effectively integrating these two approaches, Chinese manufacturing operations are creating more effective operational processes with discipline and the ability to respond to unanticipated events, for example, disruptions in the supply chain caused by sudden shifts in customer demand or supply availability.[23]

Effectively merging the best attributes of both cultures will in large part hinge on recruiting and developing talented middle management from the offshore country. Most U.S. companies do not do this well. They often bring in expatriate senior executives to their offshore operations and recruit middle management from other companies. John-Paul Ho from Crimson describes the typical situation: "Too often these expatriate executives will hire local managers according to Western views of leadership and judgments drawn from Western experience in terms of management skills. The managers hired may not be expatriates themselves, but they often come from the same offshore universities and often have lived their whole lives outside the country. The result is that managers are often not effective in providing leadership in the local cultural context."[24]

Compressing work cycles. Offshoring operations can often compress work cycles in ways not economically feasible for U.S. operations. For example, exploiting the differential in wage rates for product engineers, a major computer notebook manufacturer shaved 30 percent off the lead time required to get a new notebook model to market. To compress design and testing cycles, the Taiwanese company serving this manufacturer doubled the number of engineers working on the product development team—yet still delivered the product at one-fifth of the engineering cost that a similar staff would have incurred in the United States. Similar techniques can be used to accelerate entry into multiple national markets by configuring parallel development teams to work on different national versions simultaneously.

Time zone differences can also be leveraged to compress work cycles. The same computer notebook manufacturer developed a motherboard "around the clock." Chinese engineers did component placement and circuit layout of the board, then forwarded the design to a U.S. engineering team to perform signal integrity checking and simulation while the Chinese team slept. By the time the Chinese team had come to work the next morning, the team members could resume their design efforts with the testing feedback provided by the U.S. team. In this case, the manufacturer reduced the product design cycle by more than 60 percent.[25]

Fostering team-based competition among smaller work units.
In offshore locations, high-performance companies can create more
teams to compete on a particular project. The labor-intensive economics of these operations also allows managers to spin off new operations relative to more capital-intensive U.S. operations.

In countries like China, individuals tend to avoid overt conflict
and competition with other individuals. On the other hand, from their
schooling and work experience, Chinese workers tend to be extremely
competitive. The desire to excel is intense. The challenge is how to
harness this drive and intensity without creating cultural problems.
One way to allow confrontation and competition to occur more com-
fortably is to focus competition at the group level. By creating more
groups competing with each other, offshore operations can intensify
competition.

The right incentives and career paths can also shape competition.
American employees tend to be more individualistic, measuring success in objective terms like cash compensation. Chinese employees
tend to place more value on reputation and status within groups and
broader social networks. Thus, focusing recognition programs on group
performance and individual contributions to the group can have a significant impact on work efforts.

In one offshore software development operation, as soon as one
office exceeds thirty programmers, a new office is established to accommodate the next wave of growth. Factories in China often remain
subscale relative to comparable U.S. operations so that additional factories can be opened in other cities. This not only helps foster competition across factories, but also helps the company negotiate better
agreements with the local governments, which fear that the new factories will move to other areas.[26]

Creating more flexible supplier relationships. As we move beyond the boundaries of the individual enterprise, high-performance
organizations in offshore locations tend to create broader and more
flexible supplier relationships than are typical in the United States.
The organizations do so partly to encourage more competition among
suppliers, to exploit rapidly evolving specialization among suppliers,

and to cope with more dynamic and uncertain business environments by diversifying risk and minimizing dependence on a few suppliers. As a result, offshore manufacturing and product development operations in particular are becoming more skilled at managing pools of suppliers, which are often organized into process networks with each supplier performing a highly specialized role.

Again, high-performing U.S. companies have tended to move in the opposite direction. They generally have narrowed the number of suppliers and tightened relationships with them. Why have they taken this opposite tack? Many U.S. companies are moving in this direction because of concerns about the administrative overhead involved in coordinating activities and sharing knowledge across a broader range of suppliers. More suppliers means more people involved in managing relationships across suppliers. In the offshore locations, lower relative wages reduces such costs. U.S. companies have tried to squeeze further cost from supply-chain management by automating connections across suppliers. Until recently, this involved deploying point-to-point technology like electronic data interchange (EDI), which was costly to implement and increased exponentially in cost as the number of participants grew. Since offshore operations have less automation in general, this penalty has become less relevant.

Local Ecosystems Amplify Capability-Building Opportunities

There's another reason that offshoring locations can provide capability-building opportunities generally unavailable in more developed economies where most local business ecosystems have long since dispersed. Local business ecosystems proliferating in many offshore locations help to further amplify the efforts of companies within these ecosystems to build their own capabilities. Some of these ecosystems are now decades old. For example, from the mid-1980s on, companies from around the world congregated in the Kansai-Tokyo corridor of Japan to push the frontiers of thin-film transistor flat panel displays. Other examples are the gathering of the electronics original design manufacturers (ODMs) in Taipei and the concentration of U.S. hard disk drive companies' manufacturing operations in Singapore.[27]

In other cases, such as the business ecosystems emerging in China, these business ecosystems are much newer: the networking and communications products in Shenzhen, the semiconductor design and fabrication facilities in Shanghai, the software companies in Beijing, and motorcycle manufacturing in Chongqing.[28]

The emergence of these business ecosystems should not come as a surprise. These ecosystems are often a feature of rapidly developing economies, especially when rapidly developing technologies are also involved. In the United States, for example, we witnessed the emergence of a variety of local business ecosystems as early as the eighteenth and nineteenth centuries in areas like Lawrence, Massachusetts (textile mills), and Wall Street (financial services). In the twentieth century, Detroit (cars), Pittsburgh (steel), and Silicon Valley (electronics) gave rise to new ecosystems to drive another wave of economic growth.

We use *business ecosystem* very precisely, unlike the growing business literature that uses the phrase loosely to describe any form of collaboration across enterprises. In our context, business ecosystems refer to clusters of companies that locate their operations in close geographic proximity to each other with a defined focus on a specific type of business or technology. Within this broader focus, these companies may be quite diverse, but they are brought together by the complementary nature of their activities and, in particular, by the perceived value in accessing shared knowledge. A variety of specialized infrastructure service businesses, including finance, legal, executive recruiting, accounting, consulting, and marketing and public relations firms, help provide some of the networks that link the practitioners in these diverse businesses. In addition, other institutions like universities and government agencies may also serve both as magnets and as network nodes within the local business ecosystem.[29]

The emergence of Bangalore as a specialized ecosystem. In contrast to many of these early ecosystems in the United States, the ecosystems emerging in many offshore locations have accelerated their growth through early investment by multinational corporations. For example, Bangalore, a city of 6 million people in southern India, has emerged as a vibrant local business ecosystem focused on software and business process outsourcing services.[30] Long a cosmopolitan city, Bangalore has attracted people from many other parts of India as well as other countries, in part because of its temperate climate. Bangalore has also long been a center of engineering activity, partly because Karnataka, the state where Bangalore is located, hosts more engineering schools than does any other state in India.

Shortly after India's independence, Bangalore emerged as a center for the country's growing aeronautics and aerospace industry. The National Aerospace Laboratories, India's leading civilian R&D facility for aerospace technology, established its operations in Bangalore in 1960. Hindustan Aeronautics Limited, one of India's leading aeronautics companies, was formed in Bangalore through a merger of three preexisting companies in 1964. A vibrant high-tech industry, largely focused on serving the domestic Indian economy, grew up around these two entities over the next couple of decades.

In 1985, Texas Instruments became the first significant high-technology multinational corporation to open a major R&D center in Bangalore. Other large multinationals, including General Electric, followed suit in the early 1990s, especially in the wake of the major economic liberalization initiatives launched by the Indian government in 1991. By 1992, though, there were still only about thirty high-tech companies in Bangalore, according to Vivek Kulkarni, the former secretary for information technology and biotechnology in Karnataka.[31]

The next wave of IT investment was driven by a number of local companies that have evolved into significant players in the global software industry. In particular, Infosys and Wipro Technologies, each now generating over $1 billion in annual revenue, exploited the growing liberalization of the economy (and the related rapid decline in the cost of high-bandwidth communications cost) to focus on serving large companies overseas, especially in the United States. Beginning with relatively mundane software maintenance tasks, these companies and others have rapidly evolved their capabilities to handle large-scale end-to-end software development projects.

In a similar progression up the skill ladder, several companies established operations in Bangalore in the mid- to late 1990s to provide business process outsourcing services in the United States and Europe. Early operations of this type again focused on relatively low-skilled transcription services (e.g., in the medical and legal industry) and low-level call center activity, but since the mid-1990s, they have moved into increasingly specialized finance and accounting, human resource management, technical help desk, business analytics, and pharmaceutical drug testing services. In some cases, these business process outsourcing companies began as captive operations for large multinational companies like General Electric and Hewlett-Packard and decided to offer their services to other companies as well.

Deepening connections to Silicon Valley. Venture-capital firms like Kleiner Perkins, Sequoia, and Mayfield are driving another wave of investment activity in Bangalore. These firms are often requiring Silicon Valley software start-ups to use two geographic centers of operation—one in the United States focused on high-level architectural design, marketing, and sales and the other in Bangalore focused on software development and support. The term *micromultinationals* describes this new kind of company. These new entrepreneurial software operations in Bangalore are pushing the frontiers of software technology in areas like Web services, transaction processing platforms, and business process management. Ray Lane, a partner at Kleiner Perkins, indicates that 30 to 40 percent of that firm's recent start-ups have sent work offshore.[32] Yogen Dalal, a partner at Mayfield Fund, says that his firm will not consider funding a company without an offshoring strategy.[33]

Not only is Silicon Valley venture-capital money coming into Bangalore, but also Indian entrepreneurs are returning to Bangalore to lead new start-ups there. In fact, Indian entrepreneurs in Silicon Valley have a new expression to describe this phenomenon—B2B, or "back to Bangalore." This shift is generating considerable ferment, with over twelve hundred software and business process outsourcing services firms now operating in Bangalore, according to Vivek Kulkarni.[34]

Bangalore provides an example in microcosm of the dynamics shaping local business ecosystems in a variety of offshoring locations in both India and China. Multinational corporations and local enterprises begin to aggregate around concentrations of educational institutions. They provide the early foundations for an ecosystem encompassing a growing and diverse set of new enterprises. In many of these ecosystems organizing around digital technology, we are now beginning to see relatively strong linkages develop with Silicon Valley in the form of venture-capital investments, the establishment of facilities by larger Silicon Valley firms (e.g., Hewlett-Packard, Cisco, Oracle, Sun Microsystems, Intel, and Google), and the return of entrepreneurs—who had migrated to Silicon Valley—to set up new enterprises in Bangalore. In coastal China, we are seeing even stronger linkages form with the Taipei business ecosystem. This is a relatively new phenomenon—new ecosystems bootstrapping themselves through access to other, better-established ecosystems. Even though these new ecosystems are at relatively early stages of development, we anticipate that they will continue to play a significant role in accelerating specialized capability building in ways that will be very difficult for companies outside these local business ecosystems to replicate.

THE BOTTOM LINE

Most companies continue to significantly underestimate the potential value of offshoring, continuing to view it simply as a form of near-term wage arbitrage rather than as a powerful vehicle to accelerate capability building. Breaking this conventional mind-set will require some significant efforts. The following initiatives will start to give managers a better understanding of the current situation and help them prepare the ground for the initiatives outlined in the chapters ahead.

Experience offshoring centers firsthand. Since managers usually cannot judge from a distance the activities in such offshore locations as China and India, the entire senior management team and the board of directors of a company should focus on building a shared understanding of the potential of these locations in providing access to more specialized capabilities at lower cost. To do this, spend at least a week together, visiting key offshoring centers in China and India and meeting with executives of companies already active in these local business ecosystems as well as touring relevant operations.

During this visit, take care to understand how rapidly these local business ecosystems have evolved and are continuing to evolve. Understand that whatever you see today has dramatically changed from just a few years ago and will likely change even more radically in a few more years. Before choosing to create offshore centers, have a clear view of what is available today as well as what will likely be available in the years ahead.

Conduct an offshoring audit. You and the rest of the senior management team should conduct an offshoring audit designed to identify the business activities that are critical for the success of your company and are currently performed offshore. Quantify the significance of these activities in terms of resource commitments. Group these offshore activities into three categories based on their primary objective: local market access, access to low-wage-rate labor, and access to distinctive capabilities. Evaluate the relative success of offshoring initiatives in each of these three categories in meeting their business objectives. Where have performance shortfalls arisen, and what are the key factors contributing to these performance shortfalls? Group the major offshoring initiatives into two primary categories: outsourcing relationships and owned operations. Are there major differences in performance across these two categories? Compare the offshoring activities of your company with your three most significant competitors—if there are material differences, seek to explain them.

Assess the offshoring decision-making process. Your senior management team should clearly understand what drives the decision to go offshore, with a particular emphasis on understanding the relative importance of capability-building elements. Take the three most significant offshoring initiatives of the company, and seek to understand how senior management decided to launch these initiatives.

Were these initiatives launched as part of a systematic assessment of offshoring opportunities across the company, or were they driven by ad hoc considerations in specific parts of the company? Was there an explicit process for assessing the attractiveness of various offshore locations? To what extent did this process specifically consider the role of local business ecologies in helping to accelerate capability building? Was there any explicit comparison of the choice between creating an owned operation and working with a specialized, third-party offshore provider? If the focus was on working with an offshore service provider, was there an evaluation of potential providers in terms of their capability-building programs? Whether the offshore operation is owned or outsourced, how aggressive are the capability-building programs? Are they monitored and evaluated? More broadly, is there any ongoing process for evaluating the performance of offshoring initiatives and creating tight feedback loops for performance improvement?

3

Dynamic Specialization

The Use of Process Offshoring and Outsourcing to Accelerate Growth

I n chapter 2, we focused on the role of offshoring locations and related local business ecosystems as rich platforms for accelerated capability building. In this chapter, we will explore some of the implications for companies in terms of harnessing the power of dynamic specialization, particularly in the context of offshoring choices and strategies. As we will see, offshoring locations and related emerging markets create both opportunities and challenges for companies from more developed economies. In the course of addressing these opportunities and challenges, companies will master the techniques of process outsourcing and offshoring, which help them become more adept at dynamic specialization.

THE CASE FOR DYNAMIC SPECIALIZATION

Most executives react negatively to arguments for specialization. Specialization for many of them implies shrinkage and stagnation. Who in their right mind could want that? Successful companies grow and evolve rapidly—specialization takes companies in the opposite direction. Or does it?

Others have made the case for specialization largely in static terms. Companies should specialize for greater efficiency, so the argument goes, by shedding what they do unexceptionally well and concentrating on what they do distinctively well. But specialization based on today's capabilities is *static* specialization.[1]

Executives facing this argument often obsess over the perceived risks of specialization in a dynamic economy. If my company specializes in one area, then what happens if something disrupts the marketplace and renders my specialization worthless? Images of buggy whip manufacturers haunt these executives.[2] After all, a diversified portfolio of activities would more effectively manage the risk of business obsolescence, right? In this view, specialization favors deeper exploitation of increasingly narrower capabilities, whereas diversification favors broader exploration of new capabilities.

But, if we focus on dynamic specialization rather than static specialization, then we can turn this argument on its head. In fact, dynamic specialization may be a far superior way to accelerate the development of new capabilities and the best way to protect against business obsolescence.

By *dynamic specialization*, we mean the commitment to eliminate resources and activities that no longer differentiate the firm and to concentrate on accelerating growth from the capabilities that truly distinguish the firm in the marketplace. Consequently, firms cannot simply focus on differentiation but must also shed nondifferentiating activities.[3] But how can one grow by shedding assets and activities?[4] In fact, dynamic specialization increases the incentive, opportunity, and capability for businesses to intuit their environment and to grow rapidly through innovation. We'll use examples from a variety of industries, including financial services, computer manufacturing, telecommunications equipment, and industrial machinery, to illustrate the opportunities for growth through dynamic specialization.

Dynamic Specialization Creates Innovation Incentives

Companies that specialize in one business area cannot afford to fail in that business activity. This focus, combined with a grasp of both the opportunities and the challenges created by rapidly evolving markets, fosters throughout the organization a sense of urgency that larger, diversified companies rarely replicate. This urgency drives both faster performance improvement and alertness to potential threats from changing market needs. Companies with diversified activities often grow complacent—after all, if one element of the business fails or falls short, then other elements will probably prevail, even in very dynamic markets.

For example, a product or service company that runs a call center internally may worry about call center performance but not obsess over it, especially if the company is succeeding in other dimensions of its operations. On the other hand, a focused call center service provider operating in this highly competitive business will continually strive to reach new levels of performance. This specialized company will also have a strong incentive to search out new technologies to enhance its operations, as well as look at potential substitutes for its current services.

Dynamic Specialization Opens Innovation Opportunities

Highly specialized companies can work with a broader range of customers in their area of specialization than would be feasible for comparable operations in larger, diversified companies. This may seem paradoxical—after all, doesn't a more diversified company by definition serve a broader range of customers than a more specialized company serves?

Consider a call center embedded within a larger company. The call center really has only one "customer"—the parent company. The center is supporting only that company's products and services. No matter how good the call center operation is, that company still provides only one set of experiences to drive learning and performance improvement, whereas a specialized call center provider working with a broad range of companies can offer a more diverse set of products and services to the marketplace. This provider not only achieves greater scale but also realizes more variance in the customers served. A broad range of customers can offer much greater diversity in practices, policies, and processes as a context for the call center operator's learning and innovation. This diversity provides an excellent early-warning platform to alert the specialized provider about potential shifts in the marketplace or disruptive technologies that might threaten its business. By explicitly targeting and working with leading-edge customers, the specialized provider will likely see potential changes in its relevant market sooner than would a captive provider.

But, you might argue, the call center that is operating as a part of a larger corporation could serve other companies as well and access similar learning opportunities, right? Of course, relatively few captive operations do so. Significant internal organizational challenges confront companies that seek to make their internal operations available on the marketplace. Somebody will probably lose—either the external customers or the internal customers. Even if these challenges can be overcome, these "hybrid" operations confront an external difficulty as well. They will not attract the competitors of the parent company—thereby significantly limiting their customer reach relative to specialized, independent service providers.

Specialized software services providers like Wipro and Infosys in Bangalore are working with a diverse set of customers to rapidly enhance their own software development capabilities. The companies are implementing systematic performance feedback processes that help them continually refine their software development methodologies. More fundamentally, Wipro and Infosys are also developing insight regarding the fit between specific development methodologies and specific customer environments. Thus, not only are the methodologies themselves rapidly refined by exposure to a broad range of customers, but the choice of methodologies to provide the most value is also enhanced. Software development operations within traditional companies would typically have more limited opportunity for testing and refining their methodologies.[5]

Dynamic Specialization Builds Innovation Capabilities

Companies that are more specialized are also better positioned to act on the innovation opportunities they identify. In part, this innovative flexibility is because these companies have less organizational inertia than do companies that are less operationally focused. Executives of these specialized companies usually have more freedom than do their counterparts embedded in larger organizations. Along with enjoying more freedom, senior executives of specialized companies typically have a much deeper understanding of the operational details of their business and are therefore more able to assess the opportunities and risks of specific innovations. These executives also have organizations that need not balance the conflicting needs and interests of the other businesses. The organizations are more aligned around a single set of economics, skills, and culture. Though they may have legacy issues of their own, these executives need not confront the legacy issues of a more diversified company.

In general, specialized companies serving a broad range of customers have probably developed more loosely coupled interfaces between their own activities and the activities of their customers. These specialized companies can better modify their own operations without causing unanticipated disruptions in the operations of their customers. They can also test new approaches to their business without adverse consequences. In contrast, captive operations are generally more hardwired into the broader business processes of their parent company, so that introducing innovation is difficult.

MAKING SPECIALIZATION CHOICES

How far should companies go in their quest for specialization? As we discussed in chapter 1, companies have largely abandoned the conglomerate model of business organization in favor of more concentrated business models organized along industry lines. So, many executives may ask, haven't we already specialized? Relative to conglomerates, we certainly have, but another wave of specialization is under way. Offshoring (and related outsourcing) trends are forcing companies to accelerate a second wave of focusing initiatives, organized along business types that generally (but not entirely) correspond to the core operating processes of the firm—infrastructure management, product innovation and commercialization, and customer relationship.[6]

Broadly speaking, a number of industries, most notably financial services, pharmaceuticals, and the computer industry, have already begun to restructure in significant ways along these lines. In the credit card industry, for example, specialized transaction-processing companies handle the back-office processing, retail banks take on the role of product innovation and commercialization, and a variety of companies, ranging from Intuit to United Airlines, are offering affinity credit cards as part of their efforts to develop deeper relationships with their customers. In the pharmaceutical business, specialized biotechnology companies are taking on more of the R&D activities while the large pharmaceutical companies are focusing more on scale-intensive manufacturing and distribution roles. Offshoring is simply another trend that will reinforce and accelerate the broader unbundling of companies into more specialized and focused enterprises.

Let's look at these three business types in more detail. *Infrastructure management businesses* focus on relatively routine, high-volume business activities, like managing logistics operations, high-volume commodity manufacturing, or call center operations. We have already mentioned many of the companies that have specialized in these areas—UPS in logistics, Solectron in computer manufacturing, and Convergys in call center operations. *Product innovation and commercialization businesses* focus on the task of developing innovative new products or services and accelerating their penetration into target markets. Early examples of this kind of business focus span the spectrum, from design firms in the fashion industry to "fabless" (i.e., having no production facility) semiconductor design firms in the electronics industry. Finally, *customer relationship businesses* concentrate on identifying a target customer segment, getting to know that segment extremely well, and using this knowledge to more effectively mobilize the right bundles of third-party products and services to address the needs of their customers. In consumer markets, examples of these kinds of businesses include general practice physicians and independent financial advisers. In business markets, companies like Accenture in computers or commercial brokers in real estate provide early examples of focused customer-relationship businesses.

While we can point to examples of companies already focusing on one of these three business types, most companies today still have these three business types tightly bundled together within their enterprise walls. This is the case even though each type requires very different economics, skills, and even cultures to be successful. By tightly bundling these three businesses together, companies inevitably suboptimize the performance of one or more of the businesses. The companies therefore become vulnerable to more-focused competitors that have chosen to focus tightly on one of these business types.

This longer-term challenge confronts many companies in the offshoring arena. Many offshoring service providers have chosen to focus on one type of business—particularly in infrastructure management businesses, although interesting examples of the other two business types are also represented offshore. These providers are rapidly establishing world-class capabilities in their chosen areas of focus. More diversified companies that choose to retain these activities within their enterprise will face increasingly severe competition from companies that access these world-class capabilities from focused providers. If a diversified company chooses to shed these activities, it will lose the opportunity to differentiate in these areas and must pick other areas to develop world-class capabilities of its own.

Managers should think in terms of these three business types when making specialization choices. If they choose wisely, then they will continue to create and amplify value by accessing the specialized capabilities of other companies, many offshore. If they choose imprudently and either try too much or pick areas where they truly cannot differentiate themselves, they will destroy significant value.

Within these three business types, firms will probably specialize further. Infrastructure management businesses will probably specialize in a particular category of routine, high-volume business activities—

for example, the operation of logistics networks versus the operation of telecommunication networks. Customer relationship businesses will generally specialize in specific customer segments. Product innovation and commercialization businesses, in contrast, will specialize in certain technology or design segments. At this level, specialization choices will probably evolve over time, providing opportunities for growth by extension into adjacent capability areas.

As this unbundling of corporations proceeds, we will see new meaning in Adam Smith's views on the virtues of specialization. Dynamic specialization will reshape the business landscape, significantly improving productivity in the process. We hasten to add that this view on the unbundling of corporations does not lead to the fashionable view that businesses will fragment and that small-scale businesses will compete on an equal (or perhaps even advantaged) basis with large-scale businesses. At least two of the business types we have discussed (infrastructure management businesses and customer relationship businesses) have compelling economies of scale and scope that we believe will lead to significant concentration among large, focused enterprises.[7] Furthermore, as we will discuss in later chapters, the real opportunity for value creation will come from creative approaches to rebundling specialized firms in flexible process networks that help participants work together more effectively to get better faster.

SPECIALIZATION CHOICES IN OFFSHORING

So far, we have been talking about offshoring as a powerful vehicle for capability building. At this level, offshoring can be viewed as an opportunity. After all, most companies have an opportunity to build their own offshore facilities and adopt many of the distinctive practices emerging in these offshore locations. Even for those who lack the scale to establish their own offshore operations, offshore service providers offer access to many of these specialized capabilities. Isn't this all good news for companies in developed economies? Let's look a little closer at these two options and the related challenges.

Challenges in Establishing Owned
Operations Offshore

As they move operations offshore, companies must also assess the choice of building their own operations versus outsourcing these operations. This choice must be evaluated explicitly on the relative potential to accelerate capability building. Given the dynamic environment, the key question is not a comparison of capabilities today, but a perspective on who is in the best position to build and maintain world-class capabilities over time. Numerous factors may weigh against the natural instinct to try to keep capabilities in-house.

Few companies possess the scale or growth required to support world-class operations offshore. Scale and growth are essential to accelerated capability building both because they provide greater opportunity for specialization and because they offer attractive development and career paths for high-potential employees. For example, scale and growth enhance the ability to offer employees a broad range of experiences within compressed periods of time.

The spotty record of many early U.S. offshoring initiatives suggests that too many U.S. companies lack the management talent with the relevant experience in building these operations. They underestimate the significant execution challenges that must be addressed to make these initiatives pay off. Long-term success depends on quickly bringing together a core of experienced managers to focus on the initiative. In many cases, these operations, because of their status within their companies, will not get the best managers from inside the company or attract high-performing outside managers.

In areas like call center operations, U.S. companies have a hard time building world-class capabilities because the skill set is so specialized and so different from the skills required in other parts of the business. Often these employees are viewed, or at least perceive themselves, as second-class citizens. Moving these operations offshore can often compound the problem by adding geographic remoteness to the feeling of isolation already experienced. In contrast, specialized outsourcing businesses provide the focus and commitment required to accelerate capability building because this is their primary business. As we discussed earlier in this chapter, it will be very difficult for large companies with diversified operations to compete effectively with specialized outsourcing businesses in building capability.

If outsourcing relationships are required to access world-class offshore capabilities, these relationships must be structured in ways designed to build capability faster. Rather than negotiating and managing these relationships as short-term vendor relationships designed to get the lowest possible cost, executives of U.S. companies must view these outsourcing providers as long-term business partners and assist in any way they can in building appropriate capabilities. Dell's approach to its relationships with Taiwanese ODMs illustrates its long-term focus on capability building. Working closely with its ODM suppliers, Dell shares knowledge through a series of formal meetings occurring throughout the product life cycle. Dell structures these interactions to systematically integrate the best of its expertise with the expertise of its suppliers and, in the process, to build new capability for both sides.[8]

Of course, strategic considerations may make outsourcing options less attractive. Protection of critical intellectual property, concerns about the loss of differentiating skills, or other issues may make companies reluctant to outsource their offshore operations. In these circumstances, executives should carefully and objectively assess whether they can build and maintain world-class capabilities in their own offshore operations and, if so, then commit fully to an aggressive offshore capability-building program. If they cannot build these capabilities internally, they will become increasingly vulnerable to companies that choose to access these world-class capabilities from specialized outsourcing operations. Executives should not underestimate the challenges involved in establishing owned offshore facilities that can compete effectively over time with the capabilities offered by specialized offshore service providers.

Challenges in Relying on Specialized
Offshore Service Providers

Let's assume that a company decides to rely on specialized offshore service providers. Presumably, it has based this choice on the belief that these providers offer world-class capabilities and significant operating savings. That sounds like a great opportunity—and it is, at least in the short term.

Longer term, the range and pace of offshore capability building create their own challenges. Companies are not simply moving secondary business activities offshore. They are becoming dependent on offshore providers for core operating processes, including manufacturing, product development, and customer relationship management.

The challenge is that any company can access these same specialized offshore capabilities at comparable cost. What happens? The scope for differentiation diminishes. Also, the cost savings generated by moving operations offshore are competed away and captured by customers as more and more companies rely on offshore service providers. The result? All other things being equal (and, of course, they never are), companies relying on offshoring service providers will experience declining revenues and shrinking margins. What can be done to avoid this fate?

To continue to create value in this new world, executives must adopt a more strategic and dynamic view of offshoring. They must explicitly address two challenges. First, they must use offshoring (and related outsourcing) decisions as an opportunity to reexamine the most basic question of all: What business are we really in? To effectively leverage the specializations of others, companies must first be clear about their own areas of specialization. Second, companies must master the techniques required to access and amplify the specializations of others.

HARNESSING DYNAMIC SPECIALIZATION
OFFSHORE TO DRIVE GROWTH

Whether or not companies in developed economies choose to outsource, if they are to drive growth in their own business, they must find creative ways to harness the dynamic specialization emerging in offshore locations. As we discussed earlier, too many executives continue to view offshoring too narrowly as a way to deliver near-term operating savings without adequately pursuing opportunities to access distinctive capabilities and to drive growth.

This very set of choices and issues gets lost in today's offshoring debates. Opponents of offshoring tend to focus on near-term job loss. Supporters of offshoring take a much longer-term view, emphasizing that near-term savings will be reinvested and generate new jobs. For executives, the most interesting time horizon is the medium term, the time frame in which an individual enterprise will either create or destroy value, based on its choices around offshoring. New jobs will inevitably be created—the key question for executives is, by which companies and in which areas?

EXPANDING THE SCOPE OF
CAPABILITY BUILDING

Offshore locations in China and India are pursuing powerful capability-building approaches that are difficult to replicate in more developed economies. The emergence and rapid evolution of specialized local business ecosystems further amplifies the power of these approaches— competitors cannot easily replicate them elsewhere. These emerging ecosystems are tapping into other pools of specialization across the world. How broad or narrow is the opportunity emerging in these off-shore locations? After all, many of the early capability-building initiatives are in relatively low-skill niches like electronics assembly and low-level customer support through call centers. The evidence so far is that these niches are merely entry-level platforms for capability building.

One of the most distinctive attributes of both Chinese and Indian business executives is a pervasive sense of urgency regarding the need to catch up with the rest of the world. In our travels in these two countries, we have been struck by how often we heard a common re-frain from executives we met: "We were effectively closed out of the global economy for decades because of government trade and business restrictions, and we now must move much faster to make up for lost time." Adding to this sense of urgency is the realization there are many even lower-wage economies starting to become more active in global markets at the same time that wages in their own economies are rising through competitive pressures. These executives understand that they cannot rely solely on access to low-skill labor at low wage rates for sustainable competitive advantage.

If the executives missed this point before, then the intensifying competition within their own local business ecosystems should drive home the urgency. In Bangalore, intensifying competition for skilled programmers by offshore companies clustered together in this one city has led to a fierce bidding war for experienced talent, sharply increasing turnover rates and raising prevailing wage rates. Salaries have been rising at the rate of 20 percent per year, and skilled programmers can increase their salary by 35 percent when they switch employers.[9] If offshore companies are not careful, this intensifying competition can lead to a vicious cycle in which talent is lured away, performance drops, business erodes, and the remaining talent becomes even more vulnerable to recruiting raids by other companies. Employee turnover rates in the larger software development companies average around 10 to 15 percent per year, while in the lower-skilled call center operation the turnover rates can exceed 100 percent per year.[10] The companies most vulnerable to this vicious cycle are those that focus purely on wage rate arbitrage and ignore the need to accelerate capability building to provide attractive career paths for their employees. These competitive dynamics will ensure that the only companies to survive will be those that aggressively build capability within their organizations. The result: offshore companies are aggressively expanding the scope of capability building along multiple dimensions of business activity.

Because of the rapid pace of capability building offshore, executives of companies from developed economies must not make decisions based on snapshots of capability at any point in time. Rather, they must anticipate trajectories of capability building and position themselves to generate and capture economic value as these trajectories play out.

Moving up the skill ladder within specific operations. Even within specific areas like call center operations, there are ample opportunities to move up the skill ladder, as illustrated by eTelecare's experience. One of eTelecare's clients, a leading financial services firm in the United States, started with eTelecare on providing customer support for stored value cards like prepaid debit cards. The assignment required relatively modest call center skills. As this client became more convinced of the superior performance of eTelecare in this area, the client expanded the scope of eTelecare's call support activity to include its traveler's checks. This product area demanded much greater skills—customers usually call during high-stress times (e.g., when they have lost their traveler's checks in a foreign country), and effective response requires significant discretionary judgment by the agent (for example, wiring up to $50,000 in funds to a customer or initiating arrest procedures with local police for fraudulent use of checks). More recently, this client has transferred its call center work for its mutual fund product line, which requires sophisticated financial skills. Agents handling financial transactions of this type and providing financial advice must receive their certifications as licensed brokers by the NASD after extensive training programs. This broad range of call center work offers an additional opportunity for capability building. As a result, eTelecare can effectively attract and retain highly qualified candidates for its call center operations because it can offer a career path with diverse opportunities spanning a variety of skill levels and product areas.[11]

Expanding into adjacent activities. Companies are also creating more value from offshoring operations by expanding their offshoring initiatives into adjacent, higher-value activities. This is particularly true in product businesses with high manufacturing value added. Consider the computer industry, one of the first businesses to aggressively take advantage of offshore manufacturing opportunities.

American computer OEMs (original equipment manufacturers) began by moving relatively unskilled assembly operations offshore, often through outsourcing to electronics manufacturing service (EMS) providers like Solectron, Flextronics, and Celestica. More recently, these OEMs have increasingly relied on offshore operations to provide related services in the areas of product design, sourcing decisions, and inventory management. This movement has given rise to an entirely new category of offshore operations—the original design manufacturers. Primarily based in Taiwan, the ODMs take over the design function as well as the manufacturing operations for major computer OEMs. These companies—the top five are Hon Hai, Quanta, Compal, Asustek, and BenQ—are far less well known than their EMS counterparts.[12]

While ODMs will design products using the specifications supplied by computer OEMs, the majority of the ODMs' sales are based on products they design completely on their own, leveraging growing investments in their own R&D capability. Initially targeting low-end commodity products, these ODMs have been steadily upgrading their technology capabilities and expanding their operations in more sophisticated computer product categories. These ODMs are attractive because they offer a package of sophisticated services extending well beyond manufacturing assembly and they assume key elements of business risk, including product development risk and inventory risk, at a much lower cost than onshore U.S. operations could ever replicate.

ODMs have been rapidly taking share from more narrowly focused EMS suppliers and are generating higher levels of profitability at the same time. In 2004, the top five computer ODM companies were expected to grow by 34 percent on average, compared with an average 3 percent growth rate for the five leading EMS companies. In profitability, the same top five ODM companies are projected to have an average return on equity of 18 percent, compared with a negative average return on equity of 26 percent for the top five EMS vendors.[13]

ODMs are gaining share by offering more compelling value resulting from bringing together higher-value-added activities with offshore manufacturing assembly operations. This value not only comes from the greater savings in labor cost, but includes compression of cycle times, savings in component costs, tighter inventory management, and more adaptive supply chains, especially in smoother new-product introductions.

To deliver this value, product engineering must closely coordinate with manufacturing operations. Superior skills in design for manufacturability and specialized manufacturing processes can contribute to significant reductions in manufacturing cost through more effective product design. The distinctive skills in the aforementioned system-on-a-chip integrated circuit design in Greater China are playing a major role in reducing both component costs and manufacturing costs while increasing product reliability in a broad range of electronics products.

Combining local area network (LAN) and modem connectivity in a single chip and CD and DVD read and read-write functionality in a single chip helps personal computer ODMs aggressively deliver savings and product performance improvement to their customers.

If a company can design products more effectively in offshore locations, then why not transfer responsibility for component specification and sourcing decisions? In addition to quality and cost, a key factor in evaluating suppliers is availability and responsiveness. The staff in the offshore manufacturing operations is often in a better position to evaluate these qualities, especially with regard to local supplier options, as offshore locations like Taiwan become significant sources of technology innovation through the growth of robust local ecosystems of technology. For example, Taiwanese companies are aggressively investing in next-generation liquid crystal display (LCD) technology and may become leading-edge suppliers of this technology, not only in terms of cost, but also in performance.

As component specification and sourcing decisions migrate to offshore locations, firms often shift the responsibility for supply-chain management for these offshore locations as well. The ability to compress cycle times, optimize manufacturing operations, and deliver significant savings in inventory investment hinges on the effective coordination of activities across the supply chain. Salomon Smith Barney estimates that the top five computer ODMs achieve 35 percent faster inventory turns compared with the top five EMS vendors because of the ODMs' full responsibility for sourcing and supply-chain management.[14] In the computer industry, where prices are rapidly declining and frequent new-product introductions increase obsolescence risk, this capability of tight inventory management can be especially valuable.

Both the electronics and the apparel industries are perhaps most advanced in the widespread and systematic movement of manufacturing operations and related activities offshore. The same compelling economics and capability-building opportunities are beginning to drive similar movements in a broad range of other product manufacturing businesses, ranging from medical equipment and cellular handsets to automotive products and a variety of industrial products.

Expanding backward into the supply chain. This movement to bring together business activities offshore does not stop at the boundaries of the enterprise. Many benefits of congregating the activities within the enterprise are being further amplified when companies reconfigure the supply chain to ensure that key suppliers also join the offshore move. Clearly, it will be hard to compress cycle times and reduce inventory investments if major suppliers to offshore manufacturing operations remain in the United States. Improvements in product design through more effective collaboration with suppliers will also become more challenging. The opportunities to accelerate capability building that accrue to companies establishing offshore locations can also be enjoyed by suppliers, compounding the benefits already enjoyed by the companies leading the move to offshore operations. As John-Paul Ho of Crimson observes, "U.S. companies really limit the potential of offshoring by focusing only on their own enterprise. The real value of offshoring comes from dynamic optimization of the entire supply chain."[15]

It's not just about sourcing components or raw materials for products. One of the most neglected opportunities for additional cost savings involves local sourcing of capital equipment tooling and spare parts. Often, spare parts and tools and dies represent a significant expense item in manufacturing operations. Local suppliers may already exist or can be developed so that they deliver significant savings over traditional U.S. sourcing options, in addition to potential tax and currency benefits.

Companies making a significant commitment to moving manufacturing operations offshore must reassess their supply chain from the perspective of efficiency and effectiveness. Often, viable local suppliers can offer higher-quality and lower-cost options than can U.S. suppliers. In other cases, firms may decide to work with existing U.S. suppliers and persuade them to move the relevant operations offshore. For example, General Electric has launched a systematic program across its major business units to target key suppliers and assist them with developing offshoring programs of their own. Emerging in mainland China are large industrial parks anchored by a major product manufacturer with an array of supplier operations in the same park.

Expanding into adjacent markets. The consumer electronics industry provides an interesting example of another opportunity created by offshoring operations. So far, the focus has been on using offshore operations defensively, to improve economic performance and capability building in existing markets or businesses. Offshoring also provides an opportunity to think more aggressively about attacker strategies in adjacent markets.

We are just now seeing the first forays by traditional computer manufacturers into an array of consumer electronics markets. Gateway, in a very short time, has established a leadership position in the U.S. plasma TV market. Hewlett-Packard has entered the digital-camera market and, in a few years, carved out a 6 percent market share over market leaders like Nikon and Canon. Dell is targeting televisions and smart phones.[16]

All these companies have relied heavily on their experience with offshore ODM suppliers in their core businesses to accelerate their entry into the consumer electronics market. Having used these suppliers to strengthen their performance in their core business, these computer companies are now relying on similar relationships to target new sources of revenue. For example, Hewlett-Packard is a U.S. company working with Taiwanese ODMs to help strengthen its capability in competing with large, established Japanese camera companies that hold a significant technology advantage in important camera components such as lenses and charge-coupled device (CCD) sensors. Hewlett-Packard has expanded its digital-camera ODM relationships in Taiwan, collaborating with companies like Tekom to build on Tekom's early position in PC cameras and to deepen HP's capability in higher-performance digital cameras. Taiwanese ODMs are still strongest in the lower-end, commodity digital cameras, but have been steadily moving up the performance curve in designing and manufacturing higher-performance cameras (moving from one-megapixel cameras to four-plus-megapixel models). A rich ecosystem of component suppliers in Taiwan is strengthening the capability in major camera components like optics (Asia Optical), LCDs (AU Optronics), and complementary metal-oxide semiconductors (CMOS) sensors (ICMedia and Pixart).[17]

These early movements by U.S. computer manufacturers suggest the potential of a broader strategy to challenge the leading Japanese consumer electronics manufacturers by leveraging distinctive off-shore capabilities in Greater China. Japanese consumer electronics companies have started to move some manufacturing assembly operations to mainland China, but have generally held on tightly to higher-value-added activities like product design. The Japanese have also tended to source heavily through traditional keiretsu relationships from other Japanese suppliers, rather than exploiting the growing capability of Chinese suppliers.

While the Japanese companies continue to hold on to significant technology leadership in certain components, the technology capability landscape is shifting, especially as consumer electronics products move from analog to system-on-a-chip digital components. In some consumer product categories like DVD players, of which 75 to 85 percent are now assembled in China, this process is already well under way. Apex Digital is one of the leading companies driving this shift of DVD production to China. Based in the United States, Apex started producing DVDs in China in 1998. By 2002, it had captured 15 percent of the U.S. DVD market, leading all other vendors, including such consumer electronics heavyweights as Sony and Panasonic, in units sold. It now generates over $1 billion in revenue and is branching into other consumer electronics products like flat-panel LCD televisions.[18]

The growth of DVD assembly in China has been assisted in part by greater Japanese willingness to license key optical technology but also by the growth of a diverse, local-merchant integrated-circuit ecosystem, which provides access to a broad range of specialized integrated circuits required for the manufacture of DVD players. In China, there are now fifty-six integrated-circuit fabrication facilities in full production, about four hundred integrated-circuit design companies, and ten major wafer manufacturers. China is now the third-largest integrated-circuit manufacturer, after the United States and Japan. With integrated-circuit manufacturing growing at a rate of 42 percent per year, China is expected to become the second-largest global manufacturer of integrated circuits by 2005.[19]

EMERGING MARKETS AS A CATALYST FOR GROWTH THROUGH INNOVATION

We have focused so far on the capability-building and specialization challenges created by offshoring. There's another longer-term challenge that companies should take into account as they shape their offshoring strategy. This challenge involves the emergence and evolution of robust domestic markets in India and China.

Again, this challenge at first presents itself as an opportunity. Many companies are investing in India and China in the hope of participating in high-growth markets that may become very large over time. At a time when more-established markets in developed economies are showing signs of maturing, these high-growth markets appear particularly attractive.

In many cases, offshoring as capability building and offshoring as market participation have become intimately linked. This trend is particularly noticeable in the area of mobile telephone technology—both hardware and software, as well as services. Both China and India have already emerged as two of the largest national markets for cell phone technology in the world. Even more important, younger consumers who are early adopters of new cellular phone features and functions are heavily represented in these markets. These markets have therefore become strategically important lead markets for the introduction of new cell phone products and services. This is a major reason that some of the most advanced hardware and software engineering talent for cell phone products is now located in China. India is also developing strong software and services capability in this product category. OnMobile, for example, a company spun out of Infosys in 2000, is an entrepreneurial company focusing on developing innovative value-added services to support mobile telephone operators. One of its initiatives involves working with the Indian railway system to enable passengers to book their train tickets on their cell phones, rather than standing in long lines at a limited number of ticket centers.

Companies are discovering, however, that to effectively capture the growth potential of these markets, they must rethink both the design and the delivery of their products. Mouli Raman, the chief technology officer of OnMobile, for instance, indicated that mobile telephone network technology needed to be reduced in cost by a factor of five if it were to succeed in the Indian market.[20] Pricing to mobile network operators also must be restructured, with smaller up-front license fees and more emphasis on performance-based payments. Time to market becomes even more critical, given the early-adopter nature of the market. Many of the more established cell phone technology vendors like Nokia and Ericsson have a hard time adapting their practices to the demands of an emerging market like India, creating potential for new entrants to carve out strong footholds. In China, similar pressures in serving the local telecommunication network market have produced a new set of competitors in the global market. Chinese telecommunications equipment makers like Huawei Technologies Company and Zhongxing Telecom Ltd. are beginning to win against more-established global players like Nortel and Lucent.[21]

These patterns are recurring in market after market in both India and China. In cell phone technology, the business markets for products are perhaps even more demanding than consumer markets. Rather than marginally "localizing" global products, vendors are discovering that they must return to the drawing board and redesign products and services from the ground up to deliver both the functionality and the price points required by customers. It is generally much harder to take a product designed for a significantly higher price point and strip cost out of it while maintaining quality and functionality than it is to start over again with a new design.[22]

The experience of Cummins Engine Company in the Indian market illustrates the potential power of combining product and business process innovation to address the needs of emerging markets. Cummins is a world leader in diesel engines and generators, especially in the high-horsepower end of the market. In India, Cummins had captured a 60 percent share of this segment of the market, but it was only a marginal player in the large and high-growth, low-horsepower segment (under 100 kilowatts). Working with its external suppliers, Cummins launched a major new-product development effort seeking to design low-horsepower engines that could be sold at low price points while meeting aggressive performance targets. These targets included small footprints, high reliability, low emissions, sound atten-uation, and strong aesthetics. By packaging all components in ready-to-use "gensets," Cummins also increased the convenience of these new products for the customer. High component standardization in the products allowed Cummins to significantly shorten lead time to manufacture and deliver these engines, a key requirement for bidding on large tenders for engines. Cummins also recognized that it had to develop new, indirect distribution channels to reach target customer segments for low-horsepower engines. Among other process improve-ments, Cummins appointed more than forty-five market dealers to sup-plement its OEM channel and hired and trained mechanics to provide cost-effective service for the new products.

The results were impressive. Cummins launched a first round of new products in the 24- to 50-kilowatt range in May 2000 and then a second round of new products in the 10- to 20-kilowatt range in 2002. In the Indian market, Cummins has gained a 40 percent market share in these new product segments, and sales from these new products now account for 25 percent of the company's power-generation sales in India. These new products, even though sold at much lower price points, generate the same level of net profitability as Cummins's higher-end products. Cummins began exporting these products to other parts of Asia in 2002, and later expanded exports to Africa, Latin America, and the Middle East. Cummins may bring these products into the U.S. market in 2005.[23]

Let's take this one step further. As product and service innovation takes hold in emerging markets like India and China, what will pre-vent the innovations from challenging the much-higher-priced prod-ucts and services being sold in more-developed markets? Yes, markets always have room for premium-priced, status products. And yes, these new products and services will struggle to overcome brand loy-alty. But, as we saw in the ODM story in consumer electronics, Chi-nese manufacturers are already using established U.S. brands like Hewlett-Packard and Dell to launch their much-lower-price-point products in the U.S. market; and value-oriented retailers like Wal-Mart and Target could help unknown Asian manufacturers introduce their products in the U.S. market. After all, the imports from China sold in Wal-Mart stores already represent 1 percent of China's entire gross domestic product.[24]

As innovative products offering more value at much lower cost become available in emerging markets, we should not assume that they would remain in these markets. They may disrupt more-developed markets because existing vendors cannot cut costs from their overdesigned products as easily as new entrants can add features to their products. The vendors that choose not to compete aggressively in emerging markets like India and China now will likely find that the competition will eventually seek them out.

In thinking about offshoring and its implications, executives should consider four broad waves in the evolution of offshoring:

1. Locating operations offshore for narrow wage arbitrage and cost savings

2. Locating operations offshore to gain access to distinctive skills and to accelerate capability building

3. Locating operations offshore to target the unique and demanding needs of emerging markets

4. Driving growth in developed markets by taking innovative products and services that offer more value at lower cost from emerging markets and taking share from established vendors in developed markets

Early examples of all four waves of offshoring are already in play, but the bulk of business activity at this point is focused on navigating the transition from the first to the second wave. All companies should be anticipating the long-term opportunities and challenges created by all four waves. In this context, there are no safe havens. Opportunities, if not addressed today, will become severe challenges tomorrow.

THE BOTTOM LINE

Dynamic specialization provides an important foundation for learning and performance improvement. To build this foundation, companies must decide what businesses they are in. Most companies will resist making these difficult choices until some catalyst forces them over the edge. In the days of the conglomerates, leveraged buyout firms served as the catalyst, demonstrating that large, diversified companies were actually worth more when they were split up into more-focused entities. Today, the emergence of specialized offshoring service providers in China and India may provide a similar catalyst for the next wave of specialization. Companies that move their own operations offshore will probably struggle to replicate the performance of more-specialized providers. Those who choose to outsource as they move offshore must clarify where their own distinctive specialization resides. They must move aggressively to deepen their own capabilities so that they can continue to differentiate themselves in the market and find new sources of growth.

So, what specifically should executives do? We would suggest two actions stemming from the analysis so far.

Build alignment regarding sustaining capability advantages. After visiting offshore locations, you and the rest of the senior management team of the company must invest significant time together to develop a shared point of view regarding the capabilities the team will choose to keep internally and the greatest opportunities to access specialized capabilities externally from specialized offshore providers. In this context, discuss the company in terms of the three broad business types described earlier—infrastructure management, product innovation and commercialization, and customer relationships. In particular, be very aggressive in challenging yourselves on the rationale for maintaining inside the enterprise any infrastructure management businesses and their related capabilities. Define aggressive near-term milestones for deepening the capability in any of the business types that you decide to retain within the enterprise.

Define a strategic offshoring plan. With this context, you should then turn to shaping an aggressive long-term offshoring plan, focusing on two broad considerations. First, identify specific offshoring initiatives designed to give your company access to world-class capabilities. For activities you decide to keep within the enterprise, determine which activities are best performed offshore, and commit to investing in the appropriate organization to ensure that these groups can outperform specialized offshore providers. Be careful not to transplant your existing operations and organizations, but instead think creatively about how to harness the distinctive resources and capabilities offshore. To keep yourselves honest, designate two or three leading specialized offshore providers in the relevant activity areas as benchmarks to measure internal performance. For activities that are to be outsourced, identify the most promising offshore service providers and begin to develop business relationships with these companies. The evaluation of service providers should be heavily geared toward their talent management practices and track record in performance improvement—current performance levels are certainly relevant, but they tell only part of the story.

The strategic offshoring plan should also focus on developing privileged access to the strategically important Chinese and Indian domestic markets. As discussed earlier, these markets represent interesting near-term growth opportunities, compensating for the slower growth typical of more-developed economies. Perhaps even more important, these markets will probably seed product and service innovations that may disrupt more-developed markets. With this in mind, choose your offshoring locations according to their access to strategic domestic markets.

4

New Forms of Connection
and Coordination

Process Networks, Loose Coupling,
and Performance Fabrics

C ompanies must cultivate their own specializations to ensure that they continue to create differentiated value. But this is not sufficient. As companies become more specialized, they must increasingly rely on other companies to provide complementary capabilities. Companies must also learn how to access more effectively the resources and capabilities of other enterprises. In this context, we will discuss the growing importance of process networks as a way to effectively access specialized capability on a global scale and the role of loose coupling in helping to make these process networks scalable and flexible. We will also explore the need for performance fabrics to provide the underpinnings required for flexible networks across many enterprises.

PROCESS NETWORKS: ENSURING EFFECTIVE COORDINATION

Process networks represent a distinctive approach to organizing business activities across numerous enterprises. These networks will become the key organizational mechanism to mobilize the specialized capabilities of other companies on a global basis.

What Is a Process Network?

Networks have become a hot topic in business literature. It seems as though everyone has discovered that networks of companies are essential for business success.[1] Unfortunately, as is so often true when a topic captures the imagination of authors and audiences, the term often loses any distinctive meaning as it becomes stretched to cover an ever-broadening terrain. At their extreme, networks seem to include any interaction across enterprises, even if they amount to little more than market-based commercial transactions.

A specific form of network—which we characterize as a process network—is evolving in response to the need for more flexible access to specialized capabilities on a global scale. Process networks are designed to mobilize highly specialized companies across more than one level of an extended business process. Think of the core operating processes that exist within most companies today—supply-chain management, product innovation and commercialization, and customer relationship management—and then imagine what would be required to coordinate an extended operating process spanning multiple enterprises and multiple levels in the process. In contrast to more traditional supply-chain management or distribution-channel management activities, process networks typically extend beyond the first tier of business partners and seek to coordinate activities across multiple tiers of enterprises within a business process.

These networks represent a fundamentally different approach to organizing resources within extended business processes—rather than operating within a *push* model where resources are made available in anticipation of demand, process networks adopt a *pull* model where resources are flexibly provided in response to specific market demand. In this respect, process networks represent an institutional response to the emergence of reverse markets described earlier. Given their focus on supporting mission-critical business processes, process networks are shaped by tough performance requirements, unlike a broad range of strategic partnerships or relationships that often seem to have little substance beyond a press release.[2]

Earlier in the book, we briefly mentioned Li & Fung, a company that has organized a very successful global process network in the apparel industry. Li & Fung serves apparel designers, including retailers that sell private-label apparel. The company works with these customers to understand the requirements of their new apparel lines, including cost, quality, unit volumes, and timing of delivery.

Li & Fung then assembles a customized supply-chain process, drawing on the most appropriate specializations among its 7,500 business partners and defining the performance requirements for each participant in the supply chain. These supply chains are customized even to the level of a particular item of apparel. For example, Li & Fung may choose a supplier from Korea for a certain grade of yarn for a wool sweater, have the yarn dyed in Thailand, woven in Taiwan, cut in Bangladesh, and assembled in Mexico with a zipper supplied from Japan for delivery to U.S. distribution centers. A cotton blouse may call for a completely different set of process participants. Obviously, the logistics involved in this kind of global supply chain can also be quite complex, given the need to ship products across national borders with minimal time lags. Li & Fung works with specialized logistics companies to ensure that the overall cycle times in the supply-chain operations are as compressed as possible.

The company's business partners perform all these supply-chain activities. Li & Fung focuses on organizing the supply chain on demand to serve its customers' needs and conducting quality-assurance checks at each stage of the process to ensure that the performance requirements are being met.[3]

The participants in these process networks have clearly defined capabilities, but their roles, with one notable exception, vary, depending on the needs of the process network at any particular point in time. The one exception is the role of the process orchestrator.

Process orchestrators organize and manage process networks. Sometimes, as with Li & Fung, process orchestrators focus intensely on the orchestration task—their primary business. These pure-play orchestrators are rare, at least for now. Most process orchestrators engage in this activity as a sideline from their primary business. Hybrid orchestrators like Nike and Cisco, discussed later, are much more common.

The process orchestrator determines which company will be eligible to participate in the process network, defines the role of each participant in specific process implementations, and then acts as a guarantor to ensure that each participant performs as anticipated and is rewarded appropriately. The presence of a clearly defined orchestrator differentiates process networks from more loosely defined economic webs, where there is no gatekeeper to qualify potential participants.[4] It also distinguishes process networks from even looser aggregations of companies, where the shaper does not actively define the roles of the participants or orchestrate their activities in response to specific customer needs.[5]

Process networks can be either open or closed. If they are open, the resources of their participants can be mobilized to support the products of any company. For example, in the apparel industry, Li & Fung has organized an open process network that will serve any apparel designer or retail chain with its own private-label apparel line. Nike, also operating in the apparel industry, provides an example of a company that has organized a closed process network. This network is only available to support the production of Nike's products—it will not be available to serve the needs of other apparel designers. This does not imply that all the participants in the process network are captive to Nike. As individual companies, they may work with other apparel designers, but as participants in the process network, they only serve Nike's needs.[6]

Most process networks today are closed, organized by companies like Nike that have broader business interests and therefore are reluctant to make these networks available to other companies, especially potential competitors in their core business. At this point, there are relatively few pure-play orchestrators like Li & Fung that can provide the foundation for open process networks. For reasons we develop in chapter 5, we believe that the balance will shift over time in favor of open networks, although we will likely see a broad spectrum of options emerge and evolve.

Process networks are distinct from the specialized local business ecosystems discussed previously. The ecosystems are generally not planned—most attempts to organize such ecosystems fail. Instead, these ecosystems emerge naturally, sometimes shaped by the anchor investments of major institutions but more generally by the value that companies perceive in locating near other companies and institutions with similar or complementary capabilities. In contrast, process networks require formal orchestrators to function effectively. As discussed, specialized ecosystems usually concentrate in relatively compact geographical areas—either in an individual city or, as in Silicon Valley, in a small group of adjacent cities. Process networks represent a mechanism to access specialization on a global basis. They can become a very effective way to access the deep specialization emerging in local business ecosystems around the world. In this respect, these networks represent complementary ways of accessing capability. More generally, local business ecosystems focus on deepening specialized practices while process networks focus on organizing the activities across extended business processes—although, as we will see, this distinction will blur over time as process networks focus on accelerating capability building.

Loose Coupling: A Distinctive Process Management Approach

The concept of loose coupling is one of the key innovations in process networks. Loose coupling operates in sharp contrast to traditional business process management techniques within the enterprise. Within the enterprise, executives have developed a hardwired approach to the management of business processes extending across multiple functions within their firms—activities are specified in great detail and then monitored in equally fine detail to ensure performance. This has worked within the enterprise, although even here, as we will see, it has created some problems. Nevertheless, the hardwired approach has been responsible for delivering much of the operating savings that companies have so eagerly sought in their effort to cope with intensifying competition.

Once executives move beyond the enterprise, however, this approach begins to show its limitations. If a company has enormous market power, then it could micromanage its business partners. Other companies, however, find that the autonomy and diversity of their business partners make these process management approaches cumbersome and expensive at best and impractical at worst.

Loose coupling represents a more modular approach to process management.[7] Rather than specifying activities in great detail, loose coupling focuses on designating relatively independent modules of activity with clear "owners" that are accountable for the performance of each module. The approach concentrates on defining the performance levels that each module must meet at the interfaces connecting it with other modules. This leaves the module owners relatively free to improvise within their module as long as they can meet the specified performance requirements. The orchestrator of these loosely coupled modules typically develops a standardized way of representing performance requirements so that modules can be brought in and out of a process quickly and can collaborate with each other more effectively.[8]

Loose coupling offers several advantages in coordinating resources. First, it scales more easily than hardwired approaches. Since hardwired approaches require the detailed specification and monitoring of activities, hardwiring consumes more management resources as activities and participants increase. Second, this more scalable approach can accommodate a greater number of specialized participants. Recall the 7,500 business partners of Li & Fung—conventional hardwired approaches would simply crash in the complexity of so many players. Hardwired approaches favor fewer participants, often requiring significant compromises in access to relevant specialization. The performance of the overall process therefore improves, given the ability to access a greater number of specialized resources. Third, loose coupling effectively suits the need to coordinate across enterprises where independent participants will likely want to preserve the integrity and autonomy of their own operations. Finally, loose coupling also enhances flexibility. Orchestrators can quickly move specialized participants or modules of activity to and from the business process as customer needs change. That's why Li & Fung prefers the loose coupling approach—in the apparel industry, responding quickly to shifting customer demand is a key competitive advantage.[9] In this respect, loose coupling is a key innovation to support the move to more pull-oriented process management in contrast to push-oriented business processes.

Managers sometimes misunderstand the term *loose coupling* because *loose* is a relative term. Relationships in a loosely coupled business process are looser than hardwired relationships, but effective loose coupling actually requires the formation of far richer long-term relationships among business participants so that companies can preserve some of the benefits of hardwired managerial approaches while capturing the scalability and flexibility benefits.

Loose does not mean lax; loosely coupled systems operate to very stringent performance requirements. Li & Fung has compressed cycle times across its global apparel supply chains from months to weeks, exceeding the performance of more-hardwired competitors.

Extending the Core Operating Processes of the Enterprise

As mentioned earlier, process networks support the core operating processes of the firm—supply-chain management, product innovation and commercialization, and customer relationship networks. Consider these early examples of such global process networks in all three core operating processes.

Supply-chain management. Both Li & Fung and Nike illustrate the opportunities to create loosely coupled process networks in the orchestration of specialized suppliers of materials and production and logistics services. These networks can be quite large—both the Li & Fung and the Nike process networks encompass thousands of business partners. While these process networks seek the most specialized providers of materials and services, they also balance this quest for specialization with the search for partners optimally located to serve major regional markets. For example, to serve major apparel designers in European markets, Li & Fung has invested heavily in building relationships with business partners in Eastern Europe and the Mediterranean region.

Product innovation and commercialization. We have already discussed the rise of original design manufacturers (ODMs) in Taiwan. These companies focus on defining new products that drive down price points, both by accessing the capabilities of specialized component and subsystem suppliers and by emphasizing design for manufacturability. Taiwanese ODMs have rapidly gained share in various computer and consumer electronics categories, from desktop computers and laptops to digital still cameras and cellular telephones.

Typically, process networks focused on product innovation and commercialization have fewer participants and are much more geographically concentrated. The process networks of Taiwanese ODMs typically involve up to one hundred major technology providers, most of which are headquartered in and around Taipei. For example, in personal computers, major Taiwanese suppliers have emerged in motherboards, memory chips, video graphics cards, LCDs, CD and DVD drives, LAN and modem cards, keyboards, casings, and power supplies. For the few components like microprocessors, specialized glass products, and hard drives, where U.S. vendors usually dominate, these companies have all established major operations in Taiwan so that they can become more effective participants in the ODM process networks. This physical "co-location," supplemented by dense networks of personal relationships, enhances the potential for iterative negotiations around product design to ensure that everyone understands and is aligned around the opportunities to cost-reduce the major components and subsystems required for these commodity products. Even though much of the manufacturing of these products is migrating to coastal China, the engineering and design activities still remain heavily concentrated in Taipei.

Customer relationship management. Mention customer relationship management, and most executives will immediately focus on activities within the enterprise. When they think of customer relationships, they imagine a one-to-one relationship with each customer and, wherever possible, seek to reduce the visibility of third parties that might "dilute" that relationship. A few companies are beginning to realize that there are significant opportunities to deepen customer relationships by mobilizing the specialized resources of other companies to address specific customer needs. This collaboration marketing approach typically requires a very different mind-set and approach to organizing customer relationships.

In the technology industry, many companies help their customers identify and contact specialized complementary product and service providers. Cisco takes this one step further in its Cisco Connection Online initiative. Using a sophisticated online platform, Cisco will work with customers to define their unique needs and configure the appropriate products and services to meet those needs. It then provides relevant business partners with qualified leads and orchestrates the delivery, installation, and support of a broad range of products and services offered by its business partners. The scope of service extends across the full life cycle of a customer relationship. By maintaining an integrated view of the customer relationship and mobilizing appropriate specialized business partners to add value to its customers, Cisco has significantly deepened its relationships with these customers. It now has a much more detailed view of customer needs and positions itself as the orchestrator of a broad range of capabilities to enhance the value of its own products and services. Cisco has created a sophisticated process network to amplify the value of its own specialized products.[10]

Process networks focused on customer relationship management can encompass a large number of business participants, depending on the complexity of the products involved and the variations in user environments. For example, Cisco's process network includes thousands of business partners. Like process networks focused on supply-chain management, these process networks must access specialized resources, but they must also consider the requirement of physical proximity to customers when visits to customer sites are an integral part of the service provided. For this reason, the networks are usually more dispersed geographically compared with the process networks focused on product innovation and commercialization.

The Importance of Process Networks

Process networks represent a powerful mechanism to amplify the value of one's own specialization. They extend the core operating processes of the firm and orchestrate relevant complementary resources to add more value to the customer.

By linking together geographically separated companies, process networks provide a useful way to access the specialized capabilities emerging within local business ecosystems. For example, Li & Fung helps connect highly specialized business ecosystems like the weavers of high-fashion woolen fabrics in the Prato textile region near Florence, Italy, or the producers of advanced synthetic yarns and fabrics in Korea with a global network of fabric cutters and apparel assemblers.

As companies in developed economies wrestle with how to respond to the growing specialization emerging in offshoring centers in China and India, process networks can help turn a potential threat into an opportunity. Rather than trying to replicate the specialization available in these offshoring centers, companies can deploy or participate in process networks designed to provide more effective access to this specialization.[11] These networks in fact enhance the incentives for specialization. Companies can choose to focus more tightly on their areas of greatest competence, while remaining confident that complementary capabilities will be accessible.[12]

Companies that choose to become orchestrators of process networks can create even more value. As we have seen, there are relatively few pure-play orchestrators like Li & Fung. Like Nike and Cisco, most emerging orchestrators of process networks have their own products. These companies are using process networks to make their own products much more successful in the marketplace. As we will see, process networks have the potential to become even more powerful in amplifying value. But first, let's explore the role of performance fabrics in supporting process networks.

PERFORMANCE FABRICS:
ENABLING PROCESS NETWORKS

Process networks are enormously challenging to create, nurture, and operate. Organizing highly specialized companies from diverse backgrounds and motivating them to collaborate effectively in mission-critical business processes is obviously more difficult than aligning individuals within the boundaries of a single enterprise. What's more, the challenge multiplies as specializations become more geographically and institutionally dispersed. Process networks depend on perfor-mance fabrics to function effectively. Performance fabrics weave to-gether both business elements (e.g., techniques for building shared meaning and trust) and technology elements (e.g., architectures and interaction tools) to simplify, strengthen, and amplify relationships among relevant stakeholders across enterprises, thereby enhancing the potential for productive collaboration across a large number of specialized entities.

Performance fabrics provide the prerequisites for the effective alignment of efforts within process networks. They systematically re-duce the interaction costs that would occur if companies in a process network were all working together for the first time. Performance fab-rics weave together business elements along one dimension and tech-nology elements along a second dimension. In this chapter, we will focus primarily on the business elements of the performance fabric, particularly, shared meaning and dynamic trust. Chapter 6 will ex-plore the major technology elements that come together within per-formance fabrics. In many respects, performance fabrics across large numbers of distributed enterprises would be much less feasible with-out robust information technology support. As we discuss later in the book, we are optimistic that new generations of technology will ex-pand the reach and richness of performance fabrics. The broad out-lines of performance fabrics are defined and shaped by orchestrators, but the ultimate texture of the fabric emerges from the interactions of the process participants over time.

Building Shared Meaning

We usually take shared meaning for granted, but it often makes effective collaboration difficult, especially in loosely coupled busi-ness processes. Shared meaning exists when all parties understand specific terms in the same way—for example, do orange buyers and orange suppliers share a common method for determining ripeness? In hardwired business processes, managers specify and monitor ac-tivities closely and can intervene quickly when misunderstandings or other failures occur among process participants. In more loosely cou-pled systems, orchestrators specify the outputs required from each module, but are much less directly involved in the activities that deliver these outputs.

For this reason, orchestrators focus carefully on the task of building shared meaning. Successful orchestrators have learned that this is an iterative process that cannot be overengineered at the outset. Complete shared meaning is a chimera. Rapid iteration around shared meaning helps ensure that the meaning is truly shared, rather than imposed imperfectly on partners. The question is how to determine where shared meaning is most critical at the outset and then to expand the scope of shared meaning over time by observing where the most significant misunderstandings occur.[13]

Cisco is one of the most innovative companies in developing comprehensive learning programs to support the creation of shared meaning across its dispersed network of business partners. Tom Kelly, vice president of the Internet Learning Solutions Group at Cisco, observes that shared points of view are key to building shared meaning. With that in mind, Cisco has invested heavily in learning platforms designed to strike an effective balance between building shared points of view through structured learning as well as providing "emergency" learning modules that can help establish shared meaning in response to time-sensitive business situations. Cisco's executives realize the importance of shared meaning, but they also recognize that shared meaning is created incrementally, shaped by immediate business needs. That's one reason that Cisco makes it as easy as possible to search for and access its learning materials online and then delivers the learning material in small modules tailored to specific business needs.[14]

Without some threshold of shared meaning, reciprocal trust cannot be developed, since mutual expectations cannot be effectively communicated. So, at one level, shared meaning is a prerequisite for trust to emerge. On the other hand, companies need trust to expand the scope of shared meaning. Without trust, participants will not invest the effort required to build shared meaning. For this reason, performance fabrics cannot be completely woven at the outset; the weave must emerge over time, shaped by the interactions between all the participants of process networks.

Building Dynamic Trust

Loosely coupled process networks cannot function without reciprocal trust. In a world of growing specialization and reliance on other companies for key elements of business value, the ability to build trust quickly and effectively represents a significant source of strategic differentiation.[15] Yet, most executives seem to believe that trust is like fine wine: do the right thing, and trust will emerge in its own time— it cannot be rushed. Companies skilled at working with a broad range of business partners recognize that this is not the case; specific tools and approaches can be deployed to accelerate the building of trust.[16]

Trust is an issue that pervades all dimensions of human interaction.[17] Our focus is on trust in relationships with business partners in process networks. Many business partnerships are more opportunistic, seeking short-term benefits through collaboration and recognizing that the partners may actually end up competing with each other over time. Orchestrators of successful process networks recognize that they must build long-term, reciprocal, trust-based relationships with the participants in their networks.

Orchestrators generally depart from traditional views of trust. Conventional approaches to trust usually look backward: has the other party delivered against expectations in the past? This approach works reasonably well in static environments—the past is a reasonable predictor of the future, and the time required to establish this kind of trust is less critical. Orchestrators usually rely on forward-looking incentives as the primary mechanism to build trust quickly. Since process networks have tended to emerge in rapidly changing environments like apparel and electronics, the orchestrators of these networks are painfully aware that the past is less and less useful as a predictor of future performance. What matters is a clear assessment of current capability and the potential to accelerate capability building so that participants can adapt successfully to rapidly changing environments. Dynamic market environments require a more dynamic view of trust, giving more weight to the prospect of future capability building as a way to accelerate trust building in the near term.

Orchestrators recognize that reciprocal trust in the early stages is outcome-specific rather than generalized, as in the "trustworthiness" of an individual or institution. That is, both parties trust that each party will deliver certain outcomes as promised and that neither party will abuse privileged access to corporate resources and relationships. Agreeing on and delivering specific outcomes accelerates the building of trust.

Once the outcomes are mutually defined (i.e., meaning is shared), each party must assess the ability and willingness—the skill and will—of the other party to deliver. When assessing skill, orchestrators will often hire into their own organization the people who have managed the business operated by the process network participants. For example, in the early days of organizing its process network, Li & Fung recruited several former managers of textile plants. These seasoned executives could walk through the plant of a potential business partner and, within thirty minutes, determine the real capabilities of the plant. This deep in-house expertise emboldened Li & Fung in its ability to assess the skill of partners, even without a lengthy track record of performance.[18]

Orchestrators have learned, though, that the skill of partners is only a small factor in the trust equation, especially over time. Will can trump skill because partners, with proper motivation, will invest aggressively in building the necessary capability. On the other hand, without the appropriate will, even world-class skill makes little difference.

Will, in turn, is largely a function of incentive systems—are the parties sufficiently motivated to deliver the outcomes promised? The will to perform can be shaped by both positive incentives (rewards) and negative incentives (penalties). As we will see, rewards generally provide a more powerful and enduring form of motivation, although penalties certainly play a useful role in motivating behavior, especially on the margin when unanticipated events make execution more challenging than expected.

In thinking about positive incentives, executives often focus narrowly on near-term cash rewards. Certainly these are an important component of reward systems. Ultimately, of course, all forms of rewards for businesses must somehow be translated into cash flows, whether near term or long term.

Paradoxically, overemphasis on near-term cash rewards can actually undermine trust building, rather than accelerate it. In business, near-term cash pools available for distribution among participants is relatively fixed. If one party receives more cash benefits, then others must do with less. The resulting zero-sum game erodes trust as each party maneuvers to get as much of the fixed resource as possible, especially when the participants believe that they are conducting a onetime transaction, rather than a long-term relationship. And so orchestrators of successful process networks focus on building long-term relationships with their process participants. While very flexible in the configuration of specific processes, these networks rest on long-term relationships that deepen over time.

By focusing on the opportunity to build mutual capabilities as part of a long-term relationship, a more powerful set of incentives helps accelerate the building of trust in the near term. This focus on future-oriented capability building may diminish the relative importance of current capabilities—after all, if appropriate incentives and mechanisms are in place, existing capabilities will rapidly improve. For example, in its role as orchestrator, Nike has established systematic "tutelage" programs designed to help its production partners advance more rapidly through clearly defined capability categories. Of course, doing this effectively requires a deep knowledge of the kinds of capabilities that are most important to value creation by each business partner. Orchestrators then need to thoughtfully structure a sequence of interactions designed to facilitate joint knowledge building in areas likely to have the greatest impact on the performance of process participants. We will develop this step in more detail in chapter 5. Finally, orchestrators have to design rewards to motivate business partners to rapidly translate knowledge into tangible performance improvement.

If done well, this focus on the opportunities for joint capability building can rapidly build trust because it converts a zero-sum game into a positive-sum game. With the prospect of expanding the overall value of the process network, the participants become less focused on the near-term allocation of returns. The classic problems of opportunism and holdup that economists have warned about in business partnerships are typically the most severe where available resources are clearly defined and the only question is how these resources will be distributed.[19] As the focus shifts to the opportunity to create more aggregate value, issues of resource allocation usually diminish.

This is especially true when both parties have options. Again, somewhat paradoxically, trust becomes harder to establish and preserve when one or both parties feel that they are locked into a relationship and have no fallbacks. Lock-in raises the stakes considerably—it often becomes a bet-the-company proposition—and so the threshold for trust increases substantially. For this reason, process networks rarely seek to consume the full capacity of their participants.

The Li & Fung process network illustrates this well. As a policy, the company will seek to utilize between 30 and 70 percent of the capacity of its process participants. As orchestrator, Li & Fung believes it needs to account for at least 30 percent of the capacity of its process participants to get priority attention for its work. On the other hand, if it begins to consume more than 70 percent of the capacity, Li & Fung worries that the participants will become too dependent on it. This upper limit also helps enhance capability building since it ensures that all process participants will be exposed to a broader range of customers and business partners, thereby constantly bringing new practices into the process network.[20]

Orchestrators reinforce the positive incentives of mutual capability building by also working to reduce the potential risks created by mutual dependence. Loose coupling helps expand the range of options available in the event of unanticipated disruptions in operations. As discussed earlier, loose coupling enhances the scalability and flexibility of process networks so that other participants can be quickly plugged in when disruptions occur. Loose coupling also reduces the threshold investment required to enter into a business relationship. In more-hardwired business relationships, companies must often make significant investments to change the way they do business to conform to the specifications of their business partners. Loose coupling, with its focus on specifying outcomes rather than activities, lowers this initial investment and makes it easier to consider building trust incrementally without putting significant investment at risk.

Carefully constructed event notification systems can help provide early warning of potential performance issues, and robust exception handling procedures ensure rapid problem resolution. Performance bonds and other assurance mechanisms can provide safety nets that protect a company against economic losses created by disruptions.

These mechanisms help reduce the perceived downside risk and, in the process, strengthen the impact of positive incentives in rapidly building trust. Reputation systems administered by process orchestrators can also help punish deficient performance and reward superior performance.[21]

Trust building can be accelerated, but trust cannot be established overnight. It remains an emergent property that evolves over time. The art of accelerating trust building involves structuring appropriate migration paths that incrementally deploy the tools just described while at the same time managing risk. These tools consist of carefully constructed value exchanges designed to build capability and confidence. In each round of value exchange, one participant commits to deliver something of value to the other participant in exchange for something of value in return. These value exchanges typically evolve along two dimensions designed to manage risk exposure.

In one dimension, participants in the early rounds focus on activities of relatively limited value to manage the risk that the other party might not perform as expected. Over time, the value of the activities involved increases as more experience accumulates.

On the other dimension, participants can move from high specification of activities incrementally to much lower specification of activities, shifting focus toward definition of outputs instead. This dimension is particularly relevant when businesses need to start with high-value activities.

Depending on the business context, it may make sense to start the migration on one of these two dimensions, but most migration paths will likely look like a staircase with alternating movements across both dimensions over time. Whatever the starting point, the objective is the same: to rapidly build reciprocal trust without creating unnecessary risk.

THE BOTTOM LINE

As we have seen, process networks require performance fabrics to function effectively. Executives will need to move in parallel to develop these two elements.

Target the relevant process networks. As we recommended in chapter 3, you and the rest of the executive team should begin with some visits. Your team should arrange to visit the orchestrators of some relatively well-developed process networks. You need to develop a shared understanding of how process networks operate and the capabilities required to be a successful process orchestrator.

Within this context, assess the existing relations with business partners. To what extent do these relationships already constitute process networks rather than more limited business relationships? Keep in mind that process networks have a very specific meaning, in contrast to the popular use of vague terms like *business webs* and *ecosystems,* to describe any relationship across companies. Focus on four key questions to evaluate whether process networks already exist:

- Is there an orchestrator coordinating activity across more than two tiers of business activity?

- Are these business activities part of a core operating process— supply-chain management, customer relationship management, or product innovation and commercialization?

- Is the process management approach loosely coupled instead of hardwired?

- Are aggressive performance metrics for each business partner clearly defined and systematically used to reassess membership in the process network on an ongoing basis?

Look at other relevant process networks, and ask these questions: What process networks are already operating in relevant markets or industries? How captive or open are they? How effective are the incentive and coordination mechanisms in delivering high performance? Is your firm currently engaged in operations that could be better provided by existing process networks?

Based on these assessments, your team needs to develop a shared view of the process network opportunity, focused on these questions:

- What process networks should we target to amplify our own capabilities?

- What role should we play in these process networks—will we be the orchestrator, or will we be a participant?

- What do we need to do to create more value in these process networks?

Accelerate trust building. Pick two or three significant potential business partners, and assign a team of relevant operating managers to develop a pilot program to accelerate trust building, including a staged set of value exchanges, with these companies. As part of its efforts, this team should conduct a trust audit of two or three of the company's most important business relationships today, focusing on the following questions:

- What are the reciprocal expectations regarding outputs from the relationship?

- How clearly are the expectations communicated, and how broadly are they communicated on both sides of the relationship?

- How well has performance on both sides of the relationship lived up to expectations?

To increase the likelihood of honest feedback from business partners, you might hire an independent third party to conduct the business partner interviews.

Have the senior executives compare the program developed by this team with standard practices within the company for building relationships with business partners. Look for potential opportunities to accelerate trust building more broadly as part of a program to expand participation in process networks.

In both the trust audit and the pilot program, have the team pay particular attention to areas where the company is dictating specific activities that the business partners must perform instead of specifying outputs. Explore opportunities to build more loosely coupled relationships by shifting the focus to outputs rather than dictating activities. Identify an explicit value exchange staircase that can help accelerate trust and effectively manage potential risks at the same time.

5

Productive Friction

A Catalyst for Leveraged
Capability Building

C hapter 4 discussed the rise of process networks in helping companies access specialized capabilities on a global scale and the role of loose coupling as a mechanism to enhance the flexibility and scalability of these process networks. It also covered performance fabrics as key enablers in organizing and orchestrating process networks. Performance fabrics underlie shared meaning and dynamic trust—without these elements, loose coupling would quickly unravel and process networks would disintegrate into rivalries.

Performance fabrics and loose coupling enable not just the effective coordination of geographically distributed business participants, but also the rapid building of capability across enterprises. We call this concept *leveraged capability building* to indicate that, no matter how effectively any individual company builds its own capabilities, it will push its performance to new levels faster by forming partnerships with companies with complementary specializations. Building capabilities together requires a more systematic understanding of the mechanisms that enhance performance across broad networks of participants. The challenge of applying these mechanisms within one's own enterprise multiplies when these mechanisms must work effectively across many enterprises.

For leveraged capability building, the real test is whether companies can create relationships that accelerate the capability building of all participants. Can they amplify each party's value in the business relationship? That is, when companies leave the relationship, will they perform measurably better alone than they did before joining the collaboration? Will each have enhanced its own capabilities more effectively than it could have without any relationship? To pass this test, executives must master the new management technique of productive friction.

PRODUCTIVE FRICTION ACCELERATES
CAPABILITY BUILDING

At the beginning of the book, we briefly introduced the concept of productive friction—the third pillar of a strategy for accelerated capability building across enterprises. Productive friction increases the potential for innovation, learning, and capability building by gathering people from relevant specializations around difficult problems in settings that enhance creative problem solving. When people with diverse backgrounds, experiences, and skill sets engage with each other on real problems, the exchange usually generates friction—that is, misunderstandings and arguments—before resolution and learning occur. Often, this friction becomes dysfunctional; misunderstanding devolves into mistrust and opposing sides fixate on the distance between them rather than their common challenges. Yet, properly harnessed, friction can become very productive, accelerating learning, generating innovation, and fostering trust across diverse participants.

Our view of productive friction relates to the concept of *creative abrasion* as originally defined by Gerald Hirshberg, director of Nissan Design International, and richly developed by Dorothy Leonard, in *Wellsprings of Knowledge*.[1] These early descriptions of creative abrasion typically focus on opportunities for knowledge building at the work-group level within the enterprise. In contrast, our discussions of productive friction focus on opportunities for capability building across specialized enterprises within process networks. We also believe that the notion of productive friction can help shape new approaches to strategy, as discussed in Chapter 7.

In the business world's relentless quest for efficiency over the past several decades, most executives have become conditioned to believe that all friction is bad. After all, wasn't a frictionless economy the nirvana promised to us by the dot-com visionaries? Friction was a sign of waste and needed to be rooted out wherever it reared its ugly head. Perhaps we have been too hasty in dismissing all friction. Perhaps we should learn to embrace friction, even to seek it out and to encourage it, when it promises to provide opportunities for learning and capability building.[2] We need institutional frameworks that can help foster productive friction, and the learning that comes with it, rather than the dysfunctional friction that we too often encounter in large corporations around the world today.

Performance fabrics can help make friction productive rather than dysfunctional. Yet, performance fabrics alone cannot create productive friction. Some additional elements are required. We'll focus on four elements—performance metrics, people, prototypes, and pattern recognition—the four P's.

Performance Metrics

Productive friction is most likely to occur when performance requirements are clear, aggressive, and unconstrained. For example, in product development, teams need clear and aggressive performance targets but few if any constraints on how the product design might meet these targets. The more constraints—such as a specification that the product must use certain components—the narrower the solution space and the greater the potential for dysfunctional friction.

In this context, the design of business processes can significantly increase or reduce constraints. Traditional, hardwired business processes can coerce the participants by overspecifying actions and constraining solution spaces, whereas loosely coupled business processes can remove such constraints by specifying the performance results for each module, rather than specifying the activities within the modules.[3]

Thus, loosely coupled process networks enhance the potential for productive friction.

Action points are generally required to make these performance requirements tangible and immediate.[4] Productive friction occurs when participants must act together, perhaps introducing specific products, addressing performance shortfalls, or resolving breakdowns in operations. Without these concrete action points, people can too easily produce abstract and general answers or perspectives that imply action but actually hide profound disagreements or misunderstandings. Friction occurs precisely because participants can no longer conceal their differences and must surface them to move forward.

Consider the development of common law. Judges will issue rulings only on the specific case at hand and only after the adversaries have fully developed and confronted each other on the issues at hand. Judges rarely articulate broad principles, because they believe that good law only emerges from productive friction. Under common law, judges must issue written judgments, summarizing both the facts of the case and the rationale for their ruling—this summary becomes both an action point for the case and a *boundary object* (see later) for litigation in future cases.

People with Relevant Specialized Talent

Productive friction depends on effectively mobilizing people with relevant specializations or perspectives. When productive friction extends beyond a single enterprise, the people who must problem-solve often come from very different institutional backgrounds and possess dissimilar skills. Increasingly, customers interact deeply with vendors in an interaction that generates new insights and innovation at both the product and the process level.[5] Given the diversity of skills and backgrounds, executives should recruit *translators* and *knowledge brokers* who can bridge the knowledge gaps between the various participants.[6] In general, people engaged in productive friction must develop a deep, textured understanding of, and respect for, the relevant context for innovation as well as each other's specializations and experiences.[7]

For productive friction, simply identifying and connecting quickly with people with relevant specializations is often essential for success. As time passes, reconstructing the context of a breakdown becomes more difficult. Toyota Production System has produced such practice and process innovations because it seeks to freeze the context (even, if necessary, stopping entire assembly lines) and to rapidly mobilize the appropriate people to address problems when they arise, rather than trying to recreate the scene of the crime, so to speak. By stopping an entire assembly line until its people solve a problem, Toyota creates a compelling action point, ensuring friction and rapid resolution.[8]

Prototypes for Sharing Meaning

Productive friction requires difficult negotiations among people with very different skills, experiences, and mind-sets. These negotiations can be significantly enhanced by appropriate prototypes. We are using the term *prototypes* broadly here to describe any object that can be shared or accessed by a number of people and can help these people negotiate across the boundaries of distinct specializations. Prototypes might be anything from clay models and computer simulations to process maps and spreadsheets. As the requirements for innovation evolve, companies will likely use different kinds of prototypes to enhance productive friction.[9]

Pattern Recognition

So far, we have discussed the elements required if productive friction is to generate innovation. To build capability, participants must capture and disseminate the results of this innovation more broadly within and across enterprises. The participants need reflective processes designed to identify the practices emerging from innovation, to recognize patterns, and to increase awareness of high-impact practices across appropriate groups of practitioners.[10] For more modest forms of innovation, where similar business situations repeatedly emerge, teams often feel dismayed over having reinvented the wheel.

Often, innovations remain localized, and their economic impact marginalized, because organizations fail to recognize patterns or disseminate successful practices. Fortunately, new generations of information technology can help organizations reflect on the patterns of productive friction and to communicate emergent innovative practices. Ironically, specialization in general and orchestration in particular strengthen this dimension of friction. As discussed earlier, specialization paradoxically exposes a company to a broader range of relevant situations, enabling it to connect the dots. Rather than focusing solely on capturing local inventions, these companies can step back and spot broader patterns emerging, so that they can better assess the real significance of individual innovations.

Construction in Texas: Improvisation Within a Project

The Beck Group, headquartered in Dallas, is one of the most innovative commercial design/build companies in the United States. More broadly, construction is one of the oldest businesses and still one of the most challenging. For each major commercial construction project, hundreds of specialized, independent businesses must come together under very tight schedules and work closely together to deliver a unique and complex product. In contrast to many of the distributed process networks we described earlier, the participants in this process network come together in one location for each project. The general contractor serves as process orchestrator, recruiting appropriate participants in the network, defining roles, and specifying outputs and the sequencing of modules of activity, as well as monitoring quality along the way.

The design and construction of a large data center in Dallas illustrates the various elements that combine to generate productive friction. The client urgently needed to bring the data center on line in record time—in fact, the first phase of the data center had to operate within seven weeks. Mike Hildebrandt, the project leader from Beck, described his clear and aggressive performance target, which was shaped by a very tangible action point: "We were in a real pressure cooker—we had never delivered a facility in such a short period of time. We had to do things very differently—on the fly—to get the job done."

Mike handpicked his own team within Beck, and the company freed him from all other responsibilities so that he could devote his full time to this project. Departing from convention, Beck did not require subcontractors to bid competitively on the project, but picked them carefully according to their deep experience in the specialized capabilities for constructing this kind of facility. Because of time constraints, the subcontractors had no complete drawing of the facility, and so they met at the construction site three times weekly to refine the drawings and improvise ways to complete the job quickly and reliably. Thus, urgency removed the constraints that more detailed drawings would have imposed on a conventional project.

In addition to the rough drawings, the subcontractors used a white board in the trailer on site as a key prototype, or *boundary object*. The board became a repository for open issues and prioritized the issues to be resolved during each meeting. The placement and sequencing of mechanical and electrical systems in the data center was such an issue. The white board's predrawn grid sparked a creative approach to mapping these systems and helped compress lead times. Someone commented that the floors consisted of two-by-two-foot tiles corresponding to the grid. Mechanical systems would go under even-numbered tiles while electrical systems would go under odd-numbered tiles, so that teams from various subcontractors could work in parallel. As the idea blossomed, the subcontractors gathered excitedly around the white board and explored the ramifications on their specific jobs. Together, they visualized how this approach would roll out and agreed on their individual roles.

This innovative solution resulted because no detailed shop drawings constrained the construction team and because the relevant specialists collaborated to meet aggressive performance targets. Since the fees of each subcontractor were preset, their interests were aligned—they all wanted to finish in the shortest time and as cost-effectively as possible.

This experience highlights how three of the four P's—performance metrics, people, and prototypes—came together to create productive friction for the Beck Group. Unfortunately, the fourth P—pattern recognition—played a more modest role. Peter Beck, the head of the firm, recognized the significance of the team's improvisation and even asked the participants to present their experience to Beck's board of directors. However, Beck's customers, especially those senior managers who had always used the competitive bidding process, could not grasp the benefits of enhanced improvisation and the superior performance that resulted from the alignment of economic interests and more freedom in implementation. Absent extreme business pressure, customers naturally resort to long-accepted behaviors that they can easily justify internally. But the bid method for buying pencils in bulk is not the most efficient for developing complex projects.[11]

Motorcycles in China: Incremental Innovation

Few Westerners are familiar with Chongqing in China. Most could not even locate the city on a map. Yet, Chongqing is the home for a vibrant local business ecosystem focused on incremental innovation in motorcycle design and manufacturing. This innovation is being driven by a number of process networks focused on product innovation and commercialization. The orchestrators of these process networks are a series of entrepreneurial Chinese companies that are even less well known in Western economies—companies like Zongshen, Longxin, and Dachangjiang, which have been growing rapidly in Chongqing since the mid-1990s. Many Japanese motorcycle manufacturers would challenge how much product innovation is truly going on—they would argue that these companies are really imitators of Japanese products and are violating intellectual property rights. Without commenting on the validity of the claims regarding intellectual property rights, we believe that substantial incremental innovation occurs at the level of product architecture and redesign of components for manufacturability and savings in sourcing.

Developing a more loosely coupled product architecture. Ge Dongsheng and Takahiro Fujimoto, two economists at Tokyo University, have studied the experience of these motorcycle design process networks in Chongqing in some depth.[12] They document a fascinating new approach to product development that they describe as "localized modularization." In the traditional approach to the reverse engineering of products, a product assembler would prepare detailed design drawings of major components and subsystems and then hand these off to major suppliers for manufacturing. Under the approach used by Chongqing's privately owned motorcycle assemblers, the assemblers serve as design orchestrators, defining the key modules of the product and specifying broad performance parameters like weight and size in very rough design blueprints. They would then rely on the major suppliers to iterate with each other around more detailed designs of components and subsystems. The key to the success of this approach lies in the ability to redefine the product architecture in relatively independent functional modules. In our terminology, they moved to a more loosely coupled product architecture.

Using a supplier-driven, bottom-up design approach. Once they have implemented a more loosely coupled product architecture, process networks can harness the power of productive friction to deliver lower-cost components with satisfactory quality much more quickly than conventional top-down product-design approaches can. The product-design orchestrators maximize the potential for productive friction by defining aggressive performance objectives but leaving the implementation approach as open-ended as possible. Locating major suppliers and assemblers in the same city helps mobilize the appropriate specializations. The participants can more easily engage with each other in parallel efforts to implement new design approaches to meet the aggressive performance metrics. Informal social networks emerging in the crowded teahouses and restaurants of Chongqing (much like the coffee shops of Silicon Valley) supplement the more formal coordination of efforts across suppliers and assemblers.

Under this supplier-driven, bottom-up design approach, the major suppliers of components and subassemblies like the frame, engine, suspension, and fairing/cowling components assume much of the coordination effort among themselves. Coordination is facilitated first by the rough focal models and the modular functional architectures defined by the major assemblers. As development efforts proceed, productive friction occurs as suppliers exchange sample parts for subassembly tests. When the tests identify performance shortfalls, the relevant suppliers meet to work out appropriate design changes. Subassemblers assume orchestration responsibility for the relevant component suppliers. The major suppliers pursue a swarming approach to product design—they focus on integration issues with adjacent components only.

The evolution of competition. The advantages—and potential problems—with this innovative approach to product design are illustrated by the evolution of local competition between state-owned and privately owned assemblers and then the export-market competition between Chinese motorcycle manufacturers and established Japanese motorcycle vendors. In Chongqing, established state-owned assemblers developed joint ventures with leading Japanese motorcycle manufacturers like Honda, Yamaha, and Suzuki. These assemblers initially pursued more conventional top-down product-design approaches. With the help of their Japanese partners, the Chinese assemblers rapidly expanded the market for Chinese motorcycles. By 1993, the aggressive, state-owned companies made China the largest producer of motorcycles in the world, overtaking Japan.

When faced with intensifying competition from entrepreneurial, privately owned assemblers, the state-owned companies have been forced to increasingly shift to the localized modularization approach championed by the private assemblers. They simply could not match the time to market, cost, and quality performance, even with the assistance of leading Japanese manufacturers. The private assemblers are competing initially at an architectural level, taking the tightly integrated product architectures of major Japanese motorcycle manufacturers and defining equivalent, but loosely specified, functional modular architectures. This then sets the stage for intense competition in new component and subassembly designs focused on meeting aggressive performance targets.

In the export market, Chinese manufacturers have been rapidly gaining share, especially in emerging markets in Southeast Asia and Africa. China now accounts for 50 percent of the global production of motorcycles. The average export price of Chinese motorcycles dropped from seven hundred dollars in the late 1990s (already several hundred dollars less than equivalent Japanese models) to under two hundred dollars in 2002. Faced with this kind of aggressive price competition in high-growth markets like Vietnam, Japanese manufacturers have experienced rapid erosion of share. Honda's share of the Vietnamese motorcycle market has dropped from nearly 90 percent to 30 percent in the five years following the entry to Chinese manufacturers in 1997.[13]

Challenges created by product innovation. The advent of modular architectures for motorcycles championed by private Chinese motorcycle assemblers has not been without its downside as well. Price competition has significantly eroded profit margins of both assemblers and suppliers, calling into question whether these companies have sufficient resources to invest in product innovation that goes beyond imitation of foreign motorcycle designs. Suppliers have gained significant bargaining power relative to assemblers since they retain ownership of their own designs and can sell to competing assemblers. Many of these issues may be resolved if assemblers begin to consolidate and, in the process, assume a more active role in marketing and servicing the models that they sell.

Flat Panel Displays in Japan: "Deep" Innovation

When an economy needs deeper technology innovation, productive friction usually favors local business ecosystems as the prime mover. Process networks focused on product design assume a secondary role in hastening the commercialization of the new technology and harness more incremental, complementary product innovations. In our terminology, process networks enable *pattern recognition*, helping participants to spot the significance of specific innovations and to disseminate this insight more broadly—not just within an organization, but also across multiple enterprises participating in a process network.

The development of flat panel display (FPD) technology since the late 1980s illustrates the importance of local business ecosystems as a focal point for productive friction. This account heavily draws on the excellent book by Thomas P. Murtha, Stefanie Ann Lenway, and Jeffrey A. Hart, *Managing New Industry Creation: Global Knowledge Formation and Entrepreneurship in High Technology,* which discusses the emergence and evolution of the local business ecosystem that drove deep innovation in FPD technology.[14]

The emergence of a specialized business ecosystem. The precursor to recent generations of FPD technology—small-sized liquid crystal display (LCD) technology—took root in Japan as consumer electronics companies like Sharp and Seiko struggled from the 1960s to develop lower-cost implementations of the technology for products like watches and calculators. For this reason, an early concentration of technology expertise developed in the Kansai-Tokyo corridor of Japan. During this early period, leading Japanese companies dreamed of the use of this technology to replace cathode ray tubes in large-screen televisions. The Japanese investments in this technology attracted complementary investments by large U.S. companies like IBM, Applied Materials (a major producer of FPD-related manufacturing equipment), and Corning (a major producer of FPD-related glass materials). By the mid-1980s, a robust and highly specialized local business ecosystem consisting of major multinational corporations had formed in the Kansai-Tokyo corridor.

To become a feasible replacement for cathode ray tubes in televisions, FPD technology had to meet very aggressive size and price point targets at the product level, and these in turn implied equally aggressive yields in FPD manufacturing facilities (known as *fabs*). For this reason, major innovations needed to proceed in parallel at both the product and the manufacturing level. Since these technology companies were pushing the envelope in product and process performance, detailed design specifications emerged from collaboration among these companies and were not set rigidly in advance. In this way, productive friction enjoyed more degrees of freedom to yield innovative new designs.

Productive friction and tacit knowledge. Speed became the primary basis for competition in this technology arena. The major participants in the ecosystem raced through eight generations of technology in the ten years between 1988 (the year that fourteen-inch FPD prototypes were first demonstrated) and 1998. Given this pace of development, companies that did not make major investments in facilities in this local ecosystem were at a significant competitive disadvantage. Tacit knowledge was being rapidly generated through productive friction between the various specialized industry participants, and without a local presence, other technology companies fell further and further behind.[15]

Productive friction between the industry participants typically focused on the design and development of each new generation of fab facilities. These facilities became important boundary objects helping product designers, equipment manufacturers, and materials suppliers come together and negotiate how they could collectively achieve the aggressive performance targets for each new generation of fab facility.

Amplifying learning on a global scale. The participating multinational corporations amplified the learning from the innovation occurring in this local business ecosystem. Major U.S. companies like IBM, Applied Materials, and Corning decided to give their affiliates in this ecosystem the global responsibility for business initiatives to commercialize this technology more broadly. The decision by the major product companies like Toshiba and IBM to make their FPD products available on the merchant market to third-party integrators and OEMs helped spread these innovations to global markets more rapidly. It also helped underscore that the most promising near-term market for this innovative new technology was in the emerging notebook computer market in the early 1990s, rather than the anticipated consumer television market.

The decision to make the technology available on the merchant market also opened the way for the process networks focused on the product design of notebook computers emerging in Taiwan in the late 1990s to embrace this technology and further accelerate its commercialization. These process networks are playing an increasingly important role as they gain share in the global notebook computer market.

THE EMERGENCE AND EVOLUTION OF
LEARNING ACROSS ENTERPRISES

Executives must upgrade their skills in accessing and amplifying specialization. In this chapter, we examine how productive friction can help companies improve faster by collaborating. In fact, our strategic triad—dynamic specialization, connectivity and coordination, and leveraged capability building—unites to accelerate capability building across multiple enterprises. In determining who will create value from offshoring and related specialization, readers should seek companies that access and amplify distributed specialization.

Earlier in the book, we discussed three waves of migration that executives could pursue. The first wave—specialization—involved the move from efficiency to specialization as a firm's primary business strategy. By focusing on the next two waves separately, companies can reduce the transition costs and reap significant rewards. This is important: the mechanisms required to accelerate capability building can be staged to deliver near-term returns.

The Second Wave: Harnessing Connectivity

The next connectivity wave builds naturally on the move toward specialization and begins to lay the foundation for leveraged capability building. This is the wave moving from dynamic specialization to connectivity and coordination. It addresses the inevitable requirement to more effectively access the specialized resources of other companies as a complement to one's own specialization. As we have seen, various forms of process networks can play an important role in addressing this need. Process networks can evolve gradually from existing relationships with business partners.

The design approach of loose coupling helps make these process networks more scalable and flexible—these are important attributes as the participants become more and more specialized. Performance fabrics enable the effective functioning of process networks. We have pointed out that shared meaning and dynamic trust can and should be built incrementally. We also highlighted techniques that help accelerate the building of these two elements of performance fabrics. Although we have not yet discussed the interaction technology component of performance fabrics, new IT innovations are making more powerful interaction technology available to business (see chapter 6).

The Third Wave: Capability Building

So, executives will need loose coupling and performance fabrics to enhance the performance of process networks. These in turn will set the stage for the movement toward the next wave of change—from connectivity and coordination to leveraged capability building. Rather than simply trying to access specialized resources across multiple enterprises, aggressive companies will seek to develop techniques to accelerate capability building across process networks. It will not be enough to simply have access to existing resources. Intensifying competition will reward those that master the techniques to accelerate capability building—not only within their own enterprises, but also across participants in relevant process networks.

In this context, the elements of productive friction will become more critical. As productive friction expands within process networks, a virtuous cycle will be set in motion. New companies will be attracted to process networks because of their promise to accelerate capability building. Productive friction will help build shared meaning and trust more rapidly, and these in turn will give rise to new waves of productive friction. As the total value delivered by these process networks expands, more rewards will be available for distribution to the participants of these networks. These in turn will create even more powerful incentives to build dynamic trust and shared meaning, leading to another wave of productive friction and even more participants seeking to join the process network. Powerful network effects will expand the scope and impact of process networks on a global scale.

Over time, process networks will redefine their role. It turns out that both the loose coupling and the performance fabrics required to facilitate the coordination of resources across distributed enterprises are also prerequisites for capability building. By implementing modular approaches to process design, loose coupling helps remove the constraints on local innovation within modules. Local experiments and innovation can be deployed with less risk of unanticipated ripple effects in other parts of the business process. The shared meaning and dynamic trust established by performance fabrics also help people from diverse specializations and backgrounds to more effectively connect with each other around difficult business problems.

Rather than simply allocating existing resources more effectively, process networks will concentrate increasingly on building the capabilities of their participants. Orchestrators will reconceive their role from resource orchestration to innovation orchestration.[16] We are still at the initial stages of this third wave, although some of the early initiatives of companies like Li & Fung and Cisco suggest the potential that is ahead.

These changes will fold back on each other. Earlier in the book, we discussed the role of dynamic specialization in enhancing the potential for innovation. As process networks deepen their innovation capability, we expect that this will further accelerate the move toward even more specialization among the participants. Greater specialization will increase the potential for productive friction, which in turn will enhance the innovation capability of process networks.

These changes are likely to fold back in other interesting ways as well. So far, we have focused on accelerating capability building across enterprises. The same elements that contribute to capability building across enterprises—loose coupling, shared meaning, dynamic trust, and productive friction—are also critical to accelerating learning within the enterprise. No doubt, many skills developed in harnessing the value of process networks, performance fabrics, and productive friction across enterprises will find their way back into the enterprise.

For example, a vast shadow economy of exception handling exists within the enterprise.[17] Exception handling involves responding to unanticipated situations, such as an unexpected question from a customer, a sudden shortfall in supplier deliveries, or a technical problem in product development. Sometimes exceptions emerge from breakdowns of products and processes, but sometimes they signal unanticipated changes in the marketplace, such as new customer needs. Later in this book, we look at how exception handling can lead to innovation. Productive friction and performance fabrics will eventually transform large pockets of inefficiency into opportunities for innovation and value creation. Like many powerful trends, this one will begin on the edge of the enterprise and then gradually push into the core.

Implications for the Dynamics of Process Networks

As the shift from process orchestration to innovation orchestration occurs, it will shape the dynamics of process networks. We have already introduced the distinction between open process networks run by companies like Li & Fung and closed process networks run by companies like Nike. As leveraged capability building becomes a more significant driver of process networks, open networks will likely become increasingly advantaged relative to closed process networks. The ability to work with a broader range of customers will typically expand the opportunities for productive friction and innovation. In turn, by addressing a broader market, these open process networks will have greater opportunity to reap the rewards from this innovation.

In discussing the potential of process networks, we must be careful not to ignore some of the difficult governance and profit-distribution issues likely to arise as these networks evolve.[18] We have already suggested, however, that the rapid growth of value in these networks will typically reduce the intensity of these issues, at least in the near term. These early networks encourage their participants to continue to develop business outside the network, thus creating exits for participants concerned about unequal distribution of profits and creating incentives for orchestrators to share these profits more equally. Nevertheless, as network effects take hold and as accessible markets saturate, significant questions about profit distribution may create strain in these process networks and lead to further waves of evolution. Executives must understand that these networks are highly dynamic; many different strands interact in complex and often unpredictable ways. So business leaders should shape their decisions about participation, roles, and profit distribution according to a dynamic view of network formation and evolution and reassess these decisions regularly.

Until recently, information technology has been a significant barrier for companies seeking to access specialization in more scalable and flexible ways. Executives would be quite justified in approaching the perspectives in this chapter with considerable skepticism, given the perceived limitations of IT. Fortunately, recent innovations in IT suggest that we are about to witness a sea change in IT architectures and the advent of new tools designed to accelerate, rather than hold back, the move toward more dynamic specialization. Chapter 6 will explore this potential in greater detail.

THE BOTTOM LINE

As we have seen, performance fabrics do double duty. They facilitate loosely coupled coordination across a large number of enterprises, but they also provide the basis for productive friction to occur. Executives focused on the challenge of amplifying specialization across many enterprises must ensure that the performance fabric is strong enough to support productive friction.

Test the performance fabric. To assess the performance fabric of your process network, you need to look at your partners. Identify the five most innovative business partners of your company. Use an independent third party to assess the degree of trust that you have established with these business partners, particularly in creating a foundation for capability building.

- How willing are these business partners to discuss some of their most creative ideas with you?

- What would these business partners expect to happen if they did discuss some of their most creative ideas with you?

- Have these business partners learned from you anything that makes them better at what they do?

- Have you learned from these business partners anything that makes you better at what you do?

- What could be done to strengthen incentive structures on both sides of the relationship to motivate better performance against expectations?

- What are the specific opportunities to deepen capabilities on both sides of the relationship, and to what extent are these opportunities effectively addressed?

Reassess choices regarding process networks and business partners. Many companies typically select business partners solely on the basis of short-term considerations. Similarly, to the extent that companies participate in process networks, the choices regarding participation may have been driven by short-term motivations. As companies begin to realize the need to accelerate capability building, they must reassess their past criteria for creating and sustaining relationships. Ask the following questions about your choices regarding process networks and business partners:

- To what extent did you choose your five most significant business partners on the basis of their ability to accelerate your own long-term capability building by improvising and problem solving with you?

- To what extent do the orchestrators (they may be you or someone else) of your process networks focus on accelerating the capability building of the participants? What is their track record to date?

- Identify the five most innovative companies with capabilities complementary to yours. Do you have effective business partnerships with them? If not, why not?

Foster productive friction. Identify a particularly difficult business problem addressed by a major business partner relationship today—perhaps a product development project, a supply-chain performance issue, or a channel conflict that is undermining customer satisfaction. In terms of the four P's—performance metrics, people, prototypes, and pattern recognition—assess how the firm is handling the problem. Determine whether the firm could enhance the potential for more innovation and learning by strengthening one or more of these elements. Step back and evaluate the potential implications more broadly for efforts to foster productive friction.

6

Weaving a Performance Fabric

A Means of Adding Information Technology Faster

We have already described performance fabrics in one dimension, namely, as the shared meaning and dynamic trust that help coordinate resources in process networks and anticipate productive friction. Think of these elements as the warp of the fabric—the lengthwise fibers in a weave. As we suggested, the second dimension of a performance fabric consists of IT platforms, the woof of the fabric. This chapter explores the technology that creates extraordinary performance fabrics.

Information technology is an enabler. It can never provide strategic advantage and can sometimes actually hinder our strategy, through the legacy systems that once helped us automate activities within our enterprise and delivered critical operating savings as competition intensified. Until relatively recently, companies sought to coordinate activities across a firm's boundaries, accommodating simple document exchange but not more sophisticated coordination of processes. The cost of replacing existing systems forced us into a "big bang" mindset—it just wasn't worth doing unless executives could convince themselves that the benefits were very large.

The landscape is changing, and it's happening more rapidly than most of us had anticipated, and so we feel compelled to provide a brief overview of some of the major technologies converging for the first time to create new options for how we operate and organize our businesses. Back in the early 1990s, if we had tried to make the case that companies needed to become more specialized, coordinate their operations with many other specialized companies in global process networks, and use these process networks aggressively to get better faster by working with others, we would have been dismissed as impractical—our IT platforms were simply not up to the task. A variety of technology innovations are now coming together for the first time to deliver new capabilities for business.

Two broad developments—new architectures and new tools—are converging to enhance the potential for IT to support coordination and capability building across enterprises. New IT architectures in the form of virtualization and service-oriented architectures are emerging. In parallel, we are seeing the development of interaction tools like social software, e-learning platforms, and more versatile voice and video networks and access devices that will help people connect with each other.

Each of these developments—new architectures and new tools—is powerful in its own right. From our perspective, these developments are significant for two reasons. First, they help executives to more effectively access and mobilize the people and resources distributed across enterprise boundaries. Second, they amplify the potential for capability building across enterprise boundaries.

These architectures and tools become even more powerful when they come together to support business initiatives. Given this ability to reinforce each other, it is remarkable that distinct communities in the technology world are championing each of these technology elements and that these communities rarely talk to each other—in some cases, they are barely aware of each other. The power of these technologies can be further amplified within the broader framework of performance fabrics, where fibers from the warp and the woof weave together to create flexible but durable environments for innovation and learning.

DEPLOYING MORE FLEXIBLE
ARCHITECTURES ACROSS ENTERPRISES

Mention IT architecture to most senior executives, and they grow increasingly uncomfortable, looking for a way to quickly change the subject. This discomfort is understandable. IT architecture is a mysterious subject for most executives, one fraught with negative images. IT architectures are rigid. They often become obstacles to getting things done. Changing them is expensive and complicated. Changes inevitably demand long lead times and offer considerable uncertainty regarding any tangible business benefits.

We understand the reluctance of executives to engage in discussions on this topic. Nevertheless, we will briefly highlight recent developments in IT architectures because they are helping to enable many of the strategic business initiatives we have been discussing—dynamic specialization, connectivity and coordination, and leveraged capability building. IT architecture specifies how technology resources will be organized for the performance of tasks—much as businesses are organized by the definition of roles and relationships. Because IT was expensive in the early days of computing and delivered relatively limited performance, efficiency was the primary objective shaping the definition of IT architectures. Roles and relationships were very tightly defined to optimize the use of scarce and expensive technology resources. Flexibility was very expensive.

The word *architecture* is generally quite misleading for describing what most companies have today. Architecture calls forth images of the neat schematics of an architect who is carefully thinking through in advance all the needs of the occupants of a building and designing a structure that optimally meets these needs. Today's IT architectures are far better described with a geological metaphor—imagine geological sediments accumulating, one on top of the other, in different continents. The sediments are the various generations of IT that have been deployed in large enterprises—mainframes, minicomputers, desktop computers, servers, and mobile access devices in terms of computing power and equivalent generations of electronic networks. Rather than ripping out previous generations of technology and designing a greenfield architecture to more effectively exploit the capabilities of new technology, companies deployed new technology next to existing platforms. Where necessary, they implemented custom-designed connections to create a semblance of integration. These custom connections were also necessary to bridge departmental silos and enterprise firewalls—the equivalent of continents in the geological metaphor. Geological time is also a better way to capture the lead times required to move across these sediments and continents, especially as the complexity of the connections increased.

As the preceding description suggests, traditional IT architectures are a problem for business because of their way of coping with diversity and the growing need to connect IT resources to support business operations. Custom-designed connections are very efficient in their use of IT resources, but they are expensive to implement and even more expensive to modify over time. These connections are aptly described as *hardwired,* because of their lack of flexibility.

As we discussed at the beginning of the book, the major building blocks of IT—computing, storage, and communication networks—are continuing to advance along steep price-performance curves, delivering much more power at lower cost. These improvements in performance create new options in how to organize these components.

Virtualization Architectures:
Orchestrating Distributed Hardware Resources

Virtualization architectures take on the challenge of organizing and managing distributed hardware resources—processing, storage, and networks—so that they appear to the IT manager as if they were part of a single, integrated system. By simplifying the management task, these architectures provide flexible scalability—more resources can be added in smaller increments to fit the task at hand without significant complexity overload. The architectures also increase the utilization of hardware resources and the reliability of performance by making it easier to shift work to the resource that is most appropriate and most available.

These architectures are most advanced for data storage and network hardware, but significant progress is also occurring in applying the same virtualization principles to processing hardware. A new set of architectural standards, recently emerging under the rubric of *grid computing,* or *cluster computing,* will help make computing resources highly adaptable and, in some cases, available on demand.[1] An entire spectrum of virtualized computing architectures is emerging, including clusters comprising up to thousands of commodity computers within a single "box" or spread over an enterprise or multiple enterprises.

These options share a software overlay network designed to coordinate vast pools of hardware resources. This virtualization layer allows companies to exploit the rapidly declining prices for commodity IT hardware and to knit these small, generic units together in ways that can deliver enormous and complex power and yet deliver an order of magnitude of savings in capital expense. Without new and innovative approaches to managing these units, the total cost of ownership often swamps the cost savings of buying them. With these sophisticated overlay networks, vast pools of resources can now be managed as a single system, significantly reducing total administration costs.[2]

Virtualization architectures have become quite sophisticated within specific categories of IT hardware—for example, processing, storage, or networking. The challenge at this point is to extend these architectures to cover all forms of IT hardware and to manage them as a single virtual system. Even at this stage, however, sophisticated IT users like Charles Schwab and Google have created much more flexible and low-cost IT platforms—while handling incredibly complex tasks—using virtualization architectures.[3]

Service-Oriented Architectures: Orchestrating Software Resources

These developments support another related trend. Companies are beginning to migrate to service-oriented architectures (SOAs).[4] These architectures seek to make software resources more flexibly available. Expensive, hardwired connections across software and data harden business practices and policies. Businesspeople have come to view their existing application platforms as prisons. SOAs seek to break down these prison walls by adopting a more modular approach.

As the name suggests, service-oriented architectures represent a significant shift in the view of software—from fixed resources to shared services. Software has traditionally been viewed as functionality designed to support a specific business context and installed at the site where it will be used. In contrast, services are designed without advance knowledge of the exact uses and tasks they will be called on to support. Services are accessed when needed from wherever they reside. The location of the software becomes largely irrelevant from the user's perspective.

These new architectures use widely adopted Web services standards to help create loosely coupled connections across existing applications and databases quickly and cost-effectively.[5] As the services concept takes hold and shapes the development of new software resources, these new architectures will marginalize existing monolithic applications and encourage the development of more modular services. Like its hardware counterparts, software will begin to look more like a commodity, at least in its ability to easily and quickly switch from one module to another.

There's a catch, though. Loosely coupled connections do not cost a lot to develop, but they can consume a large amount of computing and network resources to operate. For this reason, the ability to coordinate distributed processing power is closely linked to the emergence of SOAs. If large amounts of inexpensive computer power cannot be made flexibly available to support loosely coupled connections, broad-based SOAs are not likely to be economically viable. On the other hand, the emergence of virtualization architectures could significantly accelerate the deployment of SOAs. In addition, the software overlay required to coordinate the resources in virtualization architectures in turn can help provide the foundational elements required to build robust SOAs—an interesting marriage.

Both of these emerging technology architectures depend on, and in turn help reinforce, the trend toward the increasing commoditization of hardware and software components. Commoditization of the underlying technology components allows companies to reconfigure the arrangement of these components, as business needs change. Paradoxically, this commoditization facilitates new and more flexible technology architectures that increase, rather than diminish, the potential for strategic differentiation of the businesses deploying these commodity components.[6]

Pragmatic Deployment of These New Architectures

Let us be clear: these SOAs are only now in the earliest stages of emergence. The current deployment of Web services technology represents a promising early initiative in the direction of SOAs. Web services technology—in particular, the foundation standard of eXtensible Markup Language (XML)—provides a major advance in creating ubiquitous standards for presenting data and defining the interfaces required for loosely coupled connections. However, even for companies like General Motors, Merrill Lynch, and Eastman Chemical, which have started to focus on the implications of SOAs, these architectures remain largely conceptual drawings rather than broad-based implementations. Early implementations of Web services technology tend to be very limited in scope and targeted on a specific area of the business.

Far from being a cause for skepticism about the potential of these broader architectures, these early implementations actually create optimism about the business appeal of this architecture. Not only can it provide much more flexibility in supporting business operations, but these new technology architectures can also be implemented more incrementally than could previous generations of IT architectures. Each stage of implementation can be geared to specific business initiatives and, with relatively modest investments and short lead times, can deliver tangible business value. In one respect, these new technology architectures are so powerful because they represent a true inflection point in enhanced flexibility. And because they can be implemented incrementally, the SOAs can leverage vast resources already in place by exposing these resources and making them accessible as services. This incremental power is in stark contrast to previous generations of architectures that typically required the large-scale removal of existing technology platforms and significant investment in the deployment of new resources.

To be sure, businesses must overcome many obstacles before these architectures saturate the business world. Web services standards like XML provide only a framework for developing shared meaning regarding the content of business tasks. Much hard work lies ahead for businesses to develop and refine this shared meaning over time.

SOA standards and protocols must become much more robust before they can provide the full functionality required to support all mission-critical transactions. Today, the first generation of Web services standards and protocols is used largely to automate the publishing and distribution of business information, rather than the automating of business processes like the complex and lengthy series of interactions required to execute and to close a securities transaction or a travel itinerary involving multiple travel providers.

Broadly distributed SOAs also demand new trust frameworks— both at the technology level, as in the use of robust authentication techniques, and at the business level, which focuses on shared meaning, incentive structures, and the use of risk-management programs like performance bonds. Both levels of trust frameworks will be required for the effective sharing of technology resources, especially as we move across enterprise boundaries. We are just beginning to understand how these trust frameworks must be designed and managed.[7]

This is one example of the interdependence between the business elements and the technology elements of a performance fabric. Powerful, new technology architectures require basic levels of shared meaning and trust to be viable. In turn, the incremental deployment of these technology architectures across multiple enterprises will help strengthen shared meaning and trust, creating a more receptive environment for further development of these architectures. We have written elsewhere about the role that managed service grids will play in accelerating the building of shared meaning and trust in SOAs.[8]

Loose coupling: the architectural foundation enhancing both coordination and innovation. Both virtualization architectures and SOAs embrace the concept of loose coupling as a key design principle in establishing connections across technology resources. We originally introduced the idea of loose coupling in our discussion of process networks. Loose coupling actually began as a technology concept, focusing on the opportunity to create modules of technology resources that could be flexibly orchestrated if the interfaces to these modules were appropriately designed.

Loose coupling has many virtues. The reason it is attracting so much attention now is that it offers the potential to establish more flexible and lower-cost connections across existing technology resources. This is very attractive to business executives who have invested large sums in technology platforms that are difficult to connect and that, once connected, are even more challenging to modify. Using loose coupling techniques, executives can now unearth existing resources, generating more business value from the technology investments already made.

But there's another, less obvious (at least at the outset) value to loose coupling. It powerfully encourages business innovation at two levels. First, by enhancing the ability to connect existing resources, it provides an opportunity for businesses to create new value by recombining resources. Remarkably, a lot of business innovation comes from this kind of recombination. This is especially powerful across enterprise boundaries. With these loosely coupled architectures, companies will now have an opportunity to access and assemble resources from diverse enterprises in ways that create more value for customers.

Second, loose coupling enables firms to experiment with new ways of execution at the local level. Implementing each resource as a service with standardized interfaces reduces the risk that changes in local practices will ripple across modules and create unintended consequences elsewhere. This coupling will enhance incremental innovation capabilities by supporting rapid prototyping of new products, business process redesigns, and even new business models, and by minimizing the disruption of existing business activities. As we will see, loose coupling will also enhance the ability of local work groups to improvise, which leads to more innovation.

Reversing the Evolutionary Path of Technology Architectures

Historically, information technologies have evolved inside out, from deep inside the enterprise to the edges of the enterprise. Think back to the deployment of hierarchical mainframe architectures centralized within the so-called glass house. These were replaced by more distributed client server architectures, often deployed by departments within the enterprise.

We are now seeing technology architectures evolve in a different direction—rather than continuing to proceed from the inside out, these architectures are evolving from the outside in. This is particularly the case with service-oriented architectures arising out of early deployments of Web services technology focused on connecting applications across enterprises.[9]

In fact, these SOAs are uniquely equipped to deal with the extreme challenges involved in connecting distributed and very heterogeneous technology resources operated by multiple enterprises. As these new architectures evolve from the outside in, they will begin by transforming the way enterprises connect with each other and then reorganize the technology resources operated within the enterprise.[10]

BRINGING PEOPLE BACK IN:
THE ROLE OF INTERACTION TOOLS

Flexible access to computing resources is only part of the answer. So far, information technology has largely focused on automating the formal and authorized processes of the enterprise. It has been much less helpful in supporting the emergent practices and accessing the underlying knowledge that is the real engine of business innovation. Practices and knowledge reside in people, not in data or process flow charts. By concentrating on the standardization and automation of processes, IT has sought to minimize the role of people. We have seen the business innovation pendulum swing heavily in the direction of process design and support since the 1980s. It is time to create more balance by more effectively accessing and leveraging the practices and knowledge that only people can provide—and new technology is becoming available to support this effort.

Three categories of technology are converging to easily and effectively bring people with their practices and knowledge back into the equation. Social software, e-learning tools, and new access devices combined with versatile voice, video, and data networks are amplifying the opportunities for groups of people to "collaborate on demand" and to develop more effective practices based on real-time problem solving. Certainly, without focusing on enhancing the ability to collaborate on demand, firms will rarely achieve the broader potential of business on demand or business agility.

Social Software: Mobilizing Resources to Collaborate on Demand

Social software has been around in early forms for quite some time, but it is now developing much more robust capabilities to help connect the right people at relevant times, provide them with collaboration tools, and create records of interactions that can generate insight on opportunities for innovation. Social software includes such traditional tools as e-mail (especially when enhanced by group lists) and bulletin boards, as well as more recent innovations like instant messaging (in business environments), weblogs (in their collaborative applications), wikis (collaborative workspaces), and social network analysis tools.[11] Service-oriented architectures enhance the potential of social software by making it easier to connect social software tools with existing software resources like databases, electronic documents (e.g., CAD/CAM drawings for complex systems), and analytic tools to enhance problem solving among the people mobilized by the social software.

Companies are just now beginning to deploy social software to support exception handling in their business processes. Exceptions are the big, secret underbelly of the massive enterprise applications implemented over the past couple decades. In their quest for standardization, these applications generate myriad exceptions that must be handled by people. In fact, in many operational areas of the enterprise, exception handling has become one of the largest sources of operating expense. It also represents a major source of inefficiency.

Often, the right people to handle the exception cannot be identified. Where they can be identified, a company spends significant time trying to access them and bring them together (since one person is rarely sufficient to resolve one of these exceptions). More time and effort is consumed as the company provides these people with the relevant information and analytical tools to come up with an effective resolution. In particular, effective resolution of these exceptions requires a rich understanding of the context of the exception by all the stakeholders. Once the resolution has been reached, a record of it is too often lost, so that, the next time the same exception arises, the entire resolution scramble must be repeated from scratch. This routine is not only highly inefficient; it also limits a major source of business innovation.

Exceptions are a rich seedbed for business innovation. They force employees to address unexpected challenges and opportunities and to push their practices into new directions. Ultimately, if specific exceptions reoccur frequently enough, they often lead to significant refinements in business processes themselves.

Social software can take exception handling and transform it at two levels. First, it can provide the tools to help accelerate and reduce the cost of exception handling, especially when the people required to resolve the exception are geographically distributed. Second, it can help create a repository documenting the exceptions, the people involved in resolving the exceptions, and the resolutions themselves. This repository can become an extremely valuable resource to disseminate business innovations based on the accumulated experience developed in handling a broad range of exceptions. These capabilities are valuable in all business settings, but especially across geographically widespread enterprises, for which the challenges of bringing people together quickly and capturing the learning from these interactions can be especially severe.

Appropriately implemented, SOAs rely heavily on electronic documents for coordinating resources. These documents can play a significant role in supporting exception handling by providing valuable information regarding the context of the breakdown (e.g., the process history). This information is available in a form that is both machine readable and "people readable," which helps bring computing resources and people more closely together. The richer the context available at the time of problem solving, the more opportunity for innovative business solutions.

Our belief in the business value of supporting collaboration on demand preceded the era of SOAs. Beginning in the mid-1990s, Xerox used an early implementation of social software to help its twenty thousand field customer service engineers (CSEs) share knowledge about how to tackle unexpected repair needs for its copiers and printers.[12] Xerox had provided its CSEs with extensive documentation specifying the procedures that needed to be followed to diagnose and repair equipment malfunctions. As might be expected, many situations encountered in the field were not effectively captured in these standardized procedures. The documentation was generally more effective at capturing what to do when a single fault in the equipment occurred. In practice, however, most problematic system malfunctions involved two or more faults occurring simultaneously. The documentation could not easily capture these events, since the number of possible permutations of faults was vast. It was troubleshooting these situations that consumed much of the CSEs' time.

Xerox deployed Eureka, a network-based system that relies on tips contributed from the CSEs themselves as they report on their experiences with unusual repair situations. These tips are reviewed and refined by experts in the service organization before these notes can be posted to Eureka. Customer service engineers are not paid for submitting these tips, but their names are attached to the tips they submit. The status that accrues with having tips published on Eureka appears to be more than enough to motivate active submissions. Within three years, Eureka had captured thirty thousand tips and saved Xerox an estimated $100 million a year. In addition to helping accelerate problem resolution by more effectively disseminating knowledge, Eureka now represents an important learning tool for CSEs seeking to deepen their skills. It sets the stage for product designers to use the system to better understand how to improve the performance of their products.

Eureka effectively integrates the formation of intellectual capital and social capital, making them two sides of the same coin. By encouraging the CSEs to contribute tips, Eureka transformed experience into movable knowledge that is broadly shared across a geographically distributed workforce. At the same time, by implementing a review process and requiring the author of the tip to be identified, the system also set into motion a process of building social capital. Why trust the tip? Because you know it was reviewed by your peers and, over time, because you begin to recognize certain CSEs as having more credibility than others. In many respects, Eureka anticipated the social vetting and authorship principles that are so central to the growth of the open-source movement. The reputation mechanisms embedded in Eureka (and also critical to the success of network businesses like eBay and Amazon.com) are another example of social software tools that can facilitate collaboration across large, distributed organizations.

A more recent example highlights the creative use of social software in a very traditional industry—commercial construction. Rick Davis, the CEO of DAVACO Sourcing, has created a versatile platform for reverse auctions with a twist. A recent commercial shopping center construction project drove home the value of this platform. At the outset of the project, the developer used this online platform to post a request for quotation (RFQ) for the construction of the shopping center. The developer then invited ten qualified contractors to participate in an online forum for two weeks to discuss the RFQ and suggest creative ways to value engineer the specifications to deliver a better building at lower cost. All participants could see the suggestions offered by each party, which enabled them to build on or challenge the ideas of each other. The contractors understood from the RFQ that the selection of the contractor would not be determined solely on price, but rather by a combination of factors, including creativity in value engineering the building design. In this way, all contractors had a strong incentive to participate actively in the online forum. From these discussions, many creative ideas emerged, including one counterintuitive suggestion to use more expensive roofing material to save on total cost of ownership and another proposal to use a tilt wall to eliminate expensive fire sprinkler systems. Based on these discussions, the developer then modified the design specifications for the building and used the refined RFQ to negotiate with the three most promising contractors and select the best contractor for the job (and it was not the lowest bidder—in fact, it was the contractor who made the suggestion regarding the tilt wall).[13]

This example highlights the use of social software to shape productive friction across enterprise boundaries. Aggressive performance targets were established in the initial RFQ, but the building designs were left open for modification. The result was more degrees of freedom in the participants' ability to come up with creative design ideas. The developer then recruited a qualified group of contractors and brought them together in an online forum that made it easier for a large number of geographically dispersed participants to interact. Architectural drawings and design specifications became the prototypes and boundary objects to focus discussions and idea generation. Because the interactions were all captured in the online forum, any participant could easily recognize patterns, spotting the most promising ideas and tracing their evolution through the discussions.

E-Learning: Building Shared Understanding

E-learning platforms represent a second cluster of technologies helping to amplify the role of people. These technologies include digital video, high-bandwidth internet protocol networks for video streaming, simulation tools, gaming technology, and search technology. Social software will also be increasingly embedded in e-learning platforms. Innovations in each of these technologies are leading to a fundamental rethinking of the learning process in business environments. In the past, the formal training process focused on bringing people together in centralized facilities. Now, the training material and experience can be distributed to desktops, wherever they are located.

This development leads to a second significant shift in approach. Training used to be deployed with a *push* model—people assembled for training when they were scheduled to receive it, and the corporation determined the schedule. Increasingly, training can be delivered on a *pull* model, in which training modules can be delivered on demand, when the employee determines it will be most useful to him or her, not when the company has scheduled it. This arrangement significantly helps the effectiveness of the learning process since the individual has an opportunity to apply the learning much faster if the material can be delivered on demand. Finally, the training can become more personalized, allowing employees, within some limits, to modify the sequence or schedule of the training sessions when it meets their individual needs.

These changes brought about by e-learning platforms have an even broader implication. Rather than focusing on learning processes within the enterprise, it becomes more feasible to expand the learning effort across enterprises within process networks. By enabling distributed and more personalized delivery of learning materials, companies cost-effectively reach a broader range of people.

This expanding focus of learning processes highlights another impact of e-learning. Beyond imparting specific information, the technology can be used to help shape common points of view and vocabularies across a distributed and diverse workforce. We are all familiar with the challenge of effectively communicating across the functional silos of the enterprise. This challenge becomes even more daunting when we seek to collaborate across enterprises on a global scale. Yet, some of the most promising business innovation can come from people who collaborate across functional, enterprise, and geographic boundaries to bring fresh knowledge and ways of seeing business issues to the table. E-learning can play a significant role in enhancing business innovation by enabling people from very different backgrounds to effectively collaborate, using common frameworks and vocabularies. This technology strand within the performance fabric thus helps strengthen the business strands in performance fabrics—the building of shared meaning and the related strengthening of trust.

Cisco is a leader in exploring this potential of e-learning platforms.[14] Earlier, we discussed Cisco's role as an orchestrator of process networks focused on adding value in customer relationship management. E-learning platforms are one of the key tools used by Cisco in constructing the performance fabric supporting its process network.

Over time, Cisco has developed very diverse ways of reaching and supporting its customers. The company originally relied on a direct sales force, which now numbers 9,000 employees, as the primary way to reach customers. Four thousand Cisco field system engineers also supported the sales process by providing implementation services after a sale. In an effort to reach broader segments of the market and to provide a more extensive range of specialized services, Cisco has developed relationships with 40,000 channel partners around the world, with combined sales and technical staffs of over 400,000 employees. Providing effective learning tools to such a large and distributed group of people can certainly be intimidating.

Cisco has addressed this challenge by deploying learning portals on the Internet to serve the specific learning needs of its direct sales force, its system engineers, and its channel partners. Robust search technology using metadata tags helps users of these portals locate the learning modules that are most relevant to them in any particular context.

This search capability is complemented by tailored learning roadmaps designed for various categories of users, helping to guide them to the useful learning modules at various points in their development. Cisco is working on personalizing this e-learning capability even further by understanding the specific work context of each employee and offering prescriptive recommendations regarding learning resources that might be particularly helpful. For example, if a salesperson has scheduled a sales call with a financial services company, the e-learning system might proactively suggest that the salesperson review a new learning module on new product features of particular interest to financial services companies.

These e-learning approaches have certainly yielded significant cost savings. Cisco estimates that a video-based training session that used to cost $200,000 to produce and deliver through centralized training facilities had dropped in cost by two orders of magnitude, to $2,000, in five years.

But cost savings are only a small part of the story. Other, harder-to-quantify benefits include the enhanced ability to present a common face to the customer across very diverse distribution channels. Where uniformity is required, as in standardized levels of technology expertise, Cisco's e-learning platform helps ensure this standardization while effectively deploying more specialized skills where they are required. By helping to accelerate the learning and development of the employees of its channel partners, Cisco also wins greater loyalty from its channel partners—they are far less likely to drop Cisco as a partner and more likely to provide preferential support for Cisco if they serve other vendors as well.

Cisco's e-learning platform also fosters a shared vocabulary, a set of methodologies and perspectives regarding technology architectures and evolution. This helps deepen trust and the ability to collaborate effectively. As a result, a shared vocabulary also helps increase the potential for business innovation. Given shared frameworks for understanding, employees from Cisco and its diverse channel partners can quickly assemble to address unexpected challenges or opportunities in the marketplace and come up with innovative new business approaches.

Access Devices and Networks:
Facilitating Connections

Rapid evolution of the technologies related to access devices also helps people connect with each other and with relevant resources. Smarter, more compact, and lower-cost handheld devices (telephones, PDAs, and their various hybrids) supported by higher-bandwidth, lower-cost, and more ubiquitous wireless networks are making people accessible anytime and anywhere and are arming them with the tools required to become more productive. Interestingly, the Xerox social software for its CSE organization grew out of a first experiment that equipped the field workforce with mobile radios to facilitate joint but distributed problem solving. However, this system lacked the ability to capture the information, vet it, and then disseminate it more widely.

Wireless networks are only part of the story. More broadly, the deepening capability of the Internet (in both its wired and its wireless extensions) to handle richer media like voice and video in addition to data will significantly expand our ability to connect with each other at much lower cost. We are just beginning to see voice over Internet protocols (VoIP) vendors like Vonage and Skype challenge conventional pricing structures in global voice communications. Using the Internet as their communication platform, these vendors are starting to offer standard voice telephone services on a global scale at a fraction of the cost of traditional switch-based telephone services.[15] Companies like Santa Cruz Networks are going one step further and providing scalable videoconferencing platforms that integrate real-time video, voice, and data communications over the Internet at a fraction of the cost required for more proprietary platforms.[16]

When combined with social software and e-learning platforms, more powerful access devices and networks can significantly enhance the potential for business innovation. The right people can be more quickly mobilized to address issues in real time, when the potential for real insight is often the greatest. Analytic tools, data, and the relevant experts can be brought in and overlaid for the people who are experiencing the issue firsthand and therefore have the richest understanding of the full context of the issue. Documentation of the issues and their resolution can be provided from any location, which helps close the gap between the resolution of the issue and the documenting of the resolution, and thereby improves the quality of the documentation. Innovative business solutions can be developed on the spot and then rapidly disseminated to other parts of the business (including business partners in process networks).[17]

Reshaping Approaches to Innovation

Traditional hardwired IT architectures prevent firms from supporting smaller, incremental modifications to business practices; quite the contrary, the traditional arrangement encourages executives to support costly, big-bang approaches to IT spending. Small changes to the IT architecture are so challenging that few managers can justify these efforts. On the other hand, major business initiatives with very large payoffs often can overcome the significant organizational inertia created by these IT architectures. There is only one problem: big-bang approaches to IT spending rarely deliver on their expected payoffs. Companies poured billions of dollars into enterprise application projects and Internet initiatives designed to transform the business, discovering to their dismay that the returns were smaller, longer in coming, and far more uncertain than they had anticipated.

Large-scale transformational projects require massive resources for their execution, but the returns are usually so far down the road that it is difficult to sustain the organizational commitment and momentum necessary to deliver the returns. Even where this commitment and momentum can be sustained, these projects often founder because of inadequate understanding of how work really gets done or an inability to adapt rapidly to changing market conditions.

Rapid incremental waves of business innovation, shaped by clear, near-term operational performance milestones, are generally much more effective in delivering real business value from IT investments. The new IT architectures and tools just described offer the potential to shift the focus from big-bang approaches to innovation toward a much more effective radical incrementalism. A new approach to business strategy will be helpful in focusing and amplifying the incremental innovation made possible by these new IT platforms. Chapter 7 will explore how this new approach to strategy can exploit the capability building approaches enabled by these new generations of technology.

THE BOTTOM LINE

Most companies today are still at a very early stage in the deployment of the new technology architectures and tools we have just described. Successful migration plans require a careful balance between architectural design and near-term deployments to build capability and deliver near-term business benefits. Few companies can maintain an appropriate balance between these two imperatives. To ensure that your business benefits from the full potential of these new generations of technology, you and the rest of your senior management team must become actively involved in the following four initiatives.

Develop an architectural migration plan. Companies today are still constrained by traditional, hardwired technology architectures. The CIO must take the lead in determining how the company will migrate from this traditional set of technology platforms to an architecture that effectively blends both SOA and virtualization architecture principles. Often, the IT group becomes consumed in lengthy initiatives to define new technology architectures in great detail. In the meantime, efforts to deploy new technologies are put on hold because of concerns that they might not be consistent with the new architecture.

The CIO and the broader senior management team of your company need to provide leadership to ensure that the architectural direction doesn't become too detailed too quickly. Spell out basic architectural principles early on, but focus on defining waves of architectural deployment and moving as quickly as possible to initiatives that can generate real business value. Given the general lack of experience with these new architectures, much needs to be learned along the way. Efforts to overdefine the new architecture at the outset will only delay business impact and the learning that comes from actually working with these technologies.

In defining these technology architectures, also be careful not to restrict the focus to the enterprise in isolation. Much of the early business value from these architectures will come from creating more flexible, automated connections with business partners. Determine how these new architectures will function across relevant process networks, and ensure that the initiatives taken within the enterprise are consistent with these broader architectural needs.

Launch aggressive near-term business initiatives. In parallel with the efforts to define new technology architectures, undertake a systematic business diagnostic to determine where these new architectures could have the most significant near-term business impact, given their current state of development. Again, be careful to look beyond the enterprise to find opportunities for early deployment with business partners, rather than focusing exclusively on internal deployment opportunities. Using this diagnostic, pick three of the most promising near-term opportunities and work with the IT department to design integrated business and technology initiatives to exploit these opportunities. Clearly specify aggressive operational performance goals and create tight performance feedback loops to ensure that business and IT executives maximize the learning from these early deployment initiatives.

Select early deployment targets for social software. To build similar capability with social software, identify groups of frontline staff who are wrestling with high-impact business problems. Put particular emphasis on work groups that are coming together across enterprise boundaries. In parallel, the IT organization should research the major categories of social software that are now commercially available. It should also identify existing deployments of social software within the enterprise—often these deployments are occurring without the organization's knowledge. Wherever groups have had experience with the use of this social software, the IT department should seek to understand both the patterns of deployment and the patterns of performance impact.

As high-potential target frontline work groups are identified, the IT organization should organize sessions to expose these groups to the new social software technologies available. Wherever possible, include in these sessions stories of how these technologies have been deployed in other settings to help work groups collaborate on demand. Assign a team from the IT organization to support the work group leaders in defining and deploying the appropriate social software tools to amplify the group's performance. Schedule regular debriefing sessions between the IT organization and your senior management team to deepen the understanding of the potential impact of social software and the issues that stand in the way of even greater impact.

Define a social software operating environment. In parallel, as these early deployments of social software begin to accumulate, the IT organization should focus on defining and deploying appropriate social software operating environments. Today, these social software tools largely exist as standalone tools offered by a broad array of technology vendors. While individual tools are useful, they become even more powerful when they are knit into seamless operating environments. Work groups will ultimately need tool kits tailored to specific kinds of work contexts. The IT department can play a significant role in amplifying the performance of these tools by learning from early experience with the use of these tools to create these tailored operating environments.

7

New Approaches to
Developing Strategy

Making Sense and
Making Progress

At the outset of this book, we asserted that our view of business strategy would need to change on multiple levels—reconceiving sources of strategic advantage, mastering new mechanisms and enablers to build this strategic advantage, and deploying new approaches to developing strategy. Early on, we discussed the forces that are driving us to accelerate capability building as the only sustainable edge. Most of this book has explored the variety of new mechanisms, amplifiers, and enablers now available to help us build this strategic advantage. In this final chapter, we tackle the question, What approach should companies use to develop and evolve strategies that are appropriate to their individual situations? Without an effective approach to strategy that can provide both focus and momentum, none of the strategic mechanisms we have described will deliver the value necessary. We need an engine to harness the value potential.

To provide this engine, a new approach to strategy will be required to stimulate productive friction within the senior management ranks of the enterprise. It will force key executives to come together around the most difficult issues facing the enterprise and, in the process, create a shared understanding of the key opportunities and challenges ahead and generate new insight about ways to amplify the potential of the firm's resources. By catalyzing this productive friction within the senior management team of the enterprise, strategy can also amplify the potential for productive friction in operations distributed across much broader process networks.

EVOLVING VIEWS OF STRATEGY

Since the 1970s, we have seen a pronounced drift in the view of strategy presented in management literature.[1] Business strategy as a distinct discipline emerged in the mid-1960s. At the time, it had some clear principles. Strategies were about positions and plans. The goal of strategy was to help a company identify attractive positions in relevant markets where a company could use sustainable competitive advantage to reap above-average profits for indefinite periods. Strategic analysis concentrated on understanding industry structures so that executives could target the most promising positions to occupy. Management needed to invest considerable effort and resources to understand these industry structures and strategic positions in some detail. Of course, it helped that industries were well defined and that structures remained relatively stable. Once these strategic positions were well understood, senior management could develop a strategic plan outlining in detail the sequence of operating initiatives that a company would need to take to occupy or secure its hold on strategic positions. These strategic plans typically focused on a one- to five-year time horizon.[2]

In subsequent decades, more management gurus have criticized these basic strategic principles. While the avenues of attack have varied, the general thrust has been similar. Reflecting the growing uncertainty created by intensifying competition, these critics have challenged the fundamental notion of strategies of position. In their place, the gurus have usually championed various forms of strategies of movement.[3]

Given the difficulty in anticipating outcomes in complex and rapidly changing environments, these critics question whether it makes sense to try to understand evolving industry structures, especially when the very boundaries of these industries are being fundamentally reshaped.[4] Since any advantage accruing to positions in these rapidly changing environments will probably erode quickly, perhaps executives should fixate on near-term movements designed to exploit market opportunities. In its more extreme forms, particularly prominent at the height of the dot-com bubble, this school actually questions whether there is any need for strategy. When companies are sufficiently aggressive in operational initiatives, they can hustle themselves to profitability by staying one step ahead of operational copycats. Recent interest in complexity theory has typically reinforced this broad strategic drift away from positions and plans. Complexity theory suggests that efforts to plan complex adaptive systems will probably fail. Instead, order emerges from a large number of distributed efforts, through a process of coevolution. Bottom-up emergent orders trump top-down imposed orders.[5]

Both the traditional approaches to strategy and their recent challengers have fallen short in helping executives respond to intensifying competition. Recall those broad secular business trends highlighted in chapter 1. Corporate profits as a share of gross domestic product have eroded by two-thirds since 1950 in the United States. Average lifetime on the Standard & Poor's 500 has declined by 80 percent since the mid-1940s.[6] Profitability, and even survival itself, has been challenged like never before. Current approaches to strategy have simply collapsed under this challenge. Something has to give.

SYNTHESIZING A MORE POWERFUL APPROACH TO STRATEGY

Companies are beginning to realize that speed alone is not sufficient; they also need a sense of direction. Long-term position still matters, especially as we see the growing importance of global process networks and local business ecosystems. Without some sense of long-term position, movement rapidly degenerates into random motion.

Options typically expand as change accelerates. Companies lacking a sense of direction usually fall into reactive approaches, pursuing too many options at the same time. The result is that resources are spread too thinly and performance impact diminishes because all the initiatives are under-resourced. In times of increasing uncertainty and rapid change, reactive approaches can become significant traps.

Balancing the imperatives of speed and direction requires a different strategic approach focused on two very different time horizons. A long-term horizon of five to ten years creates a background for executive decision making, and a much shorter-term horizon of six to twelve months provides the foreground, where operational and organizational initiatives play out. Without the sense of background to put events and actions into context, the foreground of the six- to twelve-month horizon, where most line executives usually operate, begins to lose coherence. This coherence especially deteriorates in the business landscape that is evolving rapidly on a global scale and with the increasing need to coordinate across enterprises.

We use the acronym FAST to summarize this strategic approach, highlighting its four primary components:

- Focus

- Accelerate

- Strengthen

- Tie it all together

Focus refers to the need to define long-term positioning strategies that will accelerate capability building across process networks and amplify the value of deeper specialization by the individual enterprise. *Accelerate* concentrates on moving more quickly in the near term to occupy these positions by supporting a limited number of six- to twelve-month operational initiatives designed to mobilize complementary resources across process networks. *Strengthen* pertains to the near-term efforts to remove roadblocks to even faster movement by strengthening the performance fabrics that support these process networks. *Tie it all together* highlights the importance of effectively integrating the three other components across networks of enterprises to amplify learning and accelerate capability building.

This approach views strategy as a form of accelerated capability building that requires the active management of competing demands across two different dimensions. On one dimension, accelerated capability building demands a careful balancing of the interests of an individual enterprise with the interests of broader process networks mobilizing complementary resources across multiple enterprises. Strategy can no longer be developed in isolation, since accelerating capability building requires effective collaboration with other enterprises in process networks. Senior managers must still maximize the long-term value of their firm, but increasingly, they must do this by enhancing the long-term value creation of relevant process networks and related specialized local business ecosystems. The orchestrators of process networks will take the lead in applying this strategic approach at the process network level, but all enterprises must craft their individual strategies according to their process networks.

The need to manage simultaneously across the two time horizons already discussed—six to twelve months versus five to ten years—represents a second dimension for the active management of competing demands. This strategic approach shifts senior management attention away from the one- to five-year horizon that consumes traditional business strategies. Ironically, all the real action and insight occurs on the peripheries of this traditional horizon—either on the six- to twelve-month horizon or on the five- to ten-year horizon. In fact, senior management spends almost no time on the one- to five-year horizon. This strategic approach also forces senior management to deal with both of these time horizons in parallel, often zooming in and out multiple times in the same discussion. The sequential approach of traditional strategies simply cannot generate the rapid learning and capability building that come from moving quickly back and forth between a very short-term operational horizon and a much longer-term strategic horizon.

Shaping the Background: The Role of Long-Term Direction

A sense of background is even more critical as environments become more turbulent and uncertain. Without this sense of background, one begins to lose any orientation or grounding. It becomes more difficult to make sense of events as they unfold. By forcing attention on the background, this strategic approach helps create meaning and focus while encouraging alertness to potentially disruptive innovations on the horizon.[7] It also helps executives choose which events and information to seek and which near-term actions will yield the greatest impact.

The background provided by the five- to ten-year horizon helps clarify for the participants the profound changes that most companies will probably experience over a five- to ten-year period. Companies should not and actually cannot describe this background in detail, because it must accommodate many permutations of the future while still providing a framework for effective resource allocations in the near term. Striking the right balance between generality and specificity at this background level—leaving ample room for exploration while ensuring effective exploitation in the near term—is an imperfect art as well as a key determinant of strategic success.

Perhaps the classic example of an effective statement of long-term direction comes from the early days of Microsoft, when the company developed a perspective communicated in two sentences: "Computing power is moving inexorably to the desktop. To succeed, we must own the desktop." It was simple and succinct, but clear enough and with enough directional force to guide the company over at least two decades of massive change in the computer industry.[8]

When Bill Gates framed this statement of long-term direction, the computer industry was in turmoil. Few people thought they could anticipate the outcome of the growing confrontation between companies championing centralized, proprietary technology architectures and a new breed of companies evangelizing distributed, open-technology architectures. Developing this kind of statement of long-term direction for the company requires a deep understanding of the likely impact of broader forces such as trends in technology performance improvement, value migration, public policy, and demographics. Executives are right to be concerned that these statements of direction are very challenging and require significant effort. Handing this off to a task force will not create any value and will consume substantial resources. The senior management team itself, under the active leadership of the CEO, must personally take this challenge on. Managers must own it at a visceral level and gather support from data gathering and analysis teams where appropriate.[9] They must, in effect, create the conditions for productive friction within their own team.

In contrast to more traditional strategy exercises, this statement of long-term direction must be brief and high level. In complex, rapidly evolving markets, any attempt to specify outcomes in detail is bound to create the illusion of greater insight and control over events than warranted. Look at the Microsoft example. Bill Gates had no illusion that he could specify the exact nature of the technology architectures that would evolve in the computer industry, but he captured the essence of the architectural trend that would in turn influence the creation of new, advantaged positions in the industry. The nature of the new, advantaged positions was also broadly stated—it had something to do with owning the desktop. The specific opportunities regarding operating systems and tie-ins to application software categories only became apparent over time. For this reason, it might be more accurate to describe these statements of long-term direction as focusing or as orienting perspectives rather than definitive statements of advantaged positions. The statements help executives know where to look, rather than telling them what they will find.

In this respect, the statements of long-term direction described here resemble the concept of strategic intent articulated by Gary Hamel and C. K. Prahalad in their compelling book, *Competing for the Future*.[10] Hamel and Prahalad certainly understood the importance of articulating the long-term direction for an enterprise in a succinct and powerful manner.[11] They also appropriately emphasized the need to focus on defining the distinctive specialization that enhances the enterprise in the long term. But their concept of strategic intent was often too enterprise-centric—it did not emphasize the need to articulate how a firm could amplify the value of this distinctive specialization by positioning the enterprise in broader networks of complementary capabilities.

Microsoft's early statement of long-term direction overlooked one critical success factor in its early business strategy: its ability to amplify the value of its internal technology capabilities on the desktop by creating powerful incentives to mobilize investment by other companies around its core operating system. The company's success hinged on its early realization that owning the desktop required two elements—strong products of its own and incentives for coinvestment by complementary resource owners. Long-term positions still matter, but only when position refers to both specialization and the local business ecosystems and process networks required to amplify value and accelerate capability building.

New schools of strategy typically fall into the complexity theory trap: they assume that the best that one can hope for in complex, rapidly evolving environments is to rapidly adapt to changing conditions. Adaptation is certainly one strategy and an element of all strategies. But in rapidly changing environments, firms have another option: *shaping strategies*. Unlike the situation in more stable markets, companies in rapidly changing environments have more strategic degrees of freedom in shaping outcomes.[12]

Even very small companies with appropriate insight can shape market evolution. Of course, they cannot determine outcomes with certainty, but with appropriate statements of long-term direction, they can increase the probability of favorable outcomes. Witness the success of Microsoft in shaping the development of the computer industry. In fact, many of the great success stories of the 1980s and 1990s —Wal-Mart and Dell come to mind—were led by strong founders who defined long-term statements of direction that helped shape the evolution of their respective markets. It may be hard to recall now, but these companies were all quite small as recently as the 1980s, yet they managed to have enormous impact in reshaping their industries.

Of course, not everyone can be, or should be, a shaper. Orchestrators of process networks are well positioned to be shapers by virtue of their specialized capabilities in mobilizing resources and accelerating capability building across enterprises. In fact, these companies' specialization is key to their ability to mobilize the resources of other companies. Li & Fung, Nike, and Cisco—leading orchestrators discussed previously—are highly specialized companies whose market success stems from leveraging the resources of their relevant process networks.

Companies pursuing more adaptive strategies will enhance their adaptive capabilities by participating in broader process networks. They will move more quickly, scale initiatives faster, and adjust course more quickly. Both shapers and adapters will amplify the value of their specialized capabilities by participating in process networks.

For companies pursuing shaping strategies, effective statements of long-term direction can do far more than help align resources within individual organizations. In environments characterized by high uncertainty, compelling statements of long-term direction can help mobilize investments by broader groups of companies in process networks. These statements often become significant shaping tools in their own right by influencing and shaping the perceptions of executives in other companies. In rapidly evolving markets, capturing mind share of executives of other companies and shaping their perceptions of opportunities and challenges can often be an effective precursor to capturing market share. Compelling statements of long-term direction can also help companies build advantaged capability-building positions as shapers of broader process networks.

At a more operational level, these statements of long-term direction also help build dynamic trust across enterprises (as well as within enterprises). As discussed, more traditional forms of trust usually look back at performance track records and reputation, whereas dynamic trust emphasizes future incentives for sustained capability building. The strength of these future incentives in turn depends on clarity of long-term direction. If a company is purely driven by short-term hustle strategies, it will struggle to attract potential business partners to longer-term capability-building opportunities, and conversely, it will retreat from these opportunities itself.

MANAGING IN THE FOREGROUND:
BUILDING MOMENTUM THROUGH FOCUS

While the company is developing and refining this shared understanding of longer-term direction, senior management must focus on a different time horizon, which is shaped by a second key business question: What can we do in the near term (six to twelve months) that will help us accelerate movement toward this longer-term direction? In part, this question forces executives to identify and focus on the most promising two to three operational initiatives that can deliver tangible near-term performance impact and significantly move the company in the longer-term direction. In answering this question, executives should be careful to avoid the trap of focusing solely on operational initiatives within the enterprise. Certainly, the most powerful near-term operational initiatives increasingly require the effective mobilization of complementary resources in relevant process networks.

In focusing on near-term impact, it is important to differentiate between financial and operational measures of impact. Financial measures are generally less helpful, because they are lagging indicators of performance. In defining the milestones to measure the progress of critical near-term operational initiatives, senior management is far better off focusing on the operational levers that ultimately drive financial performance. These usually leading indicators provide a more granular view of the performance of the business. For example, if the operational initiative seeks deeper penetration of a target market segment, management should focus on measures like new-customer acquisition rates, repeat-purchase rates, and retention rates rather than revenue growth.

These two to three operational initiatives differ from the notion of experimentation that has become quite popular in strategy writing.[13] As major resource commitments by the corporation, these initiatives complement, and often reinforce, each other rather than act as experiments to cover multiple options. These initiatives are designed to significantly affect the operating performance of the company over a six- to twelve-month horizon.

In that they are designed to yield near-term operational impact, the initiatives are incremental. They may or may not be incremental in the sense of supporting the previous trajectory of the business. If the business—like Wal-Mart—is performing well and does not confront significant market discontinuities over the next five to ten years, then this type of incremental initiative may be appropriate. On the other hand, if the business is not performing well or confronts significant discontinuities on the horizon—as illustrated by Kodak—the near-term operating initiatives may represent a significant departure from the current trajectory of the business. In this case, it is particularly important to focus on key operating metrics that measure progress, rather than on financial measures.

Financial measures usually increase inertia. The core business will always appear to have a higher priority than new business initiatives, given its much greater impact on overall corporate financial performance. For example, in a $10 billion business, a 1 percent improvement in performance in the core business will bring $100 million to the bottom line—swamping any possible impact that an entirely new business might generate over the same period. Operating metrics like the delivery of an operating prototype of a new product and the acquisition of initial reference customers focus senior management attention on the necessary milestones that new businesses must meet to become viable.

Often, the near-term operating initiatives will represent a mix of both the improvement of core business performance and fundamental new-business-creation initiatives, in the spirit of the "ambidextrous corporation" described by Michael Tushman and Charles O'Reilly in *Winning Through Innovation*.[14] When creating fundamentally new businesses, some initiatives may extend well beyond the individual enterprise, including efforts to create or to join entirely new process networks. Senior executives in companies supporting both types of operating initiatives must manage the inevitable deep tensions. The mind-sets, cultures, risk profiles, and metrics required to succeed in both types of operating initiatives are fundamentally different. Senior executives must anticipate and honor these tensions, rather than applying a single management model in both areas.

At one level, our emphasis on the growing importance of specialization may appear inconsistent with the pursuit of fundamental new-business-creation initiatives. We can resolve this paradox by clarifying the relevant dimensions of specialization for particular companies. Specialization does not necessarily mean small. In fact, as we discussed, specialization increasingly will be a prerequisite for effective scale and profitable growth. For example, Li & Fung is already a quite large company, even though it is highly specialized in the orchestration of process networks, particularly in the apparel industry. To grow further, the company could apply its deep specialization in the orchestration of process networks to related markets. Li & Fung believes it has distinctive expertise in orchestrating distributed, labor-intensive operations for product categories in which the product life cycles are relatively short. The company is therefore investing in building process networks in product categories like toys and furniture with many of the same characteristics as apparel. These initiatives involve fundamentally new businesses at one level, yet at another level they are logical extensions of Li & Fung's specialized process network orchestration business.

On the same six- to twelve-month time horizon, executives must ask what organizational barriers are preventing companies in their relevant process networks from moving even faster in the near term. They can then determine a set of near-term organizational initiatives designed to strengthen the capability to support even more aggressive, near-term operating initiatives. In practice, these initiatives will likely strengthen both the warp and the woof of the performance fabrics required for process networks to function effectively. Recall that the warp of the performance fabrics focuses on critical business elements like shared meaning and dynamic trust while the woof of the fabrics involves the deployment of more loosely coupled IT architectures and tools designed to facilitate more flexible collaboration across enterprises.

Harnessing Productive Friction to Generate Strategic Insight

Overall, constant iteration between these two time horizons helps accelerate both learning and performance improvement. Tight feedback loops help translate the learning into near-term action. The background provided by a longer-term direction for the business helps provide grounding, orientation, and sense making—all key requirements for effective learning. The foreground, with its emphasis on near-term action, helps companies rapidly develop real-world experience, generating valuable insight into what works and what doesn't, in both the near term and the longer term. The emphasis on near-term action also pushes companies to translate learning into action quickly and thereby repeat the learning cycle. In effect, the foreground created by this strategic approach provides a basis for single-loop learning while the background provides the context for double-loop learning. In this case, double-loop learning refers to the opportunity to reflect on, and refine where appropriate, the basic assumptions and frames of reference that guide management decisions.[15] This learning dimension makes this strategic approach particularly valuable in times of rapid change and high uncertainty—speed of learning becomes a key strategic advantage in these environments.

This strategic approach generates sustained productive friction at multiple levels. Within the senior management of an enterprise, this approach forces executives to confront difficult and fundamental business issues in a structured manner. The newer approaches to strategy that abandon any longer-term perspective on the business have become quite appealing, partly because they allow executives to avoid difficult questions. What business are we really in? It's too soon to decide—the business will emerge from our near-term actions. Where do we need to ensure a critical mass of resources in the near term? It's not clear—we must fund lots of experiments to find out. To executives who are overwhelmed by uncertainty outside and organizational politics inside, these answers can be very seductive, but they are also dangerous. Strategic insight and sustained performance improvement come from asking hard questions and demanding focused attention to open issues.

This strategic approach, with its emphasis on accelerating capability building through process networks, also forces executives to expand their horizons beyond their own enterprise. For example, executives using this strategic approach would align around the following issues:

- What process networks would be most effective in amplifying the value of our own specialized capabilities?

- How can we best access distinctive skills emerging in distributed local business ecosystems across the globe?

- Which business partners would be most helpful in accelerating our own capability building?

- Are we learning as much as we can from the process networks we participate in?

- What is the right balance between captive and noncaptive relationships to enhance the learning capabilities of our partners and of our own company?

- How can we structure relationships to minimize the risks of holdup and nonperformance?

At another level, this strategic approach also helps promote productive friction throughout the organization and across process networks. As we discussed, productive friction depends on a number of elements, including clear and aggressive performance metrics and effective pattern recognition to drive performance feedback loops. This strategic approach defines aggressive near-term operational performance metrics to accelerate movement toward longer-term strategic destinations. As participants within process networks struggle to achieve these near-term performance objectives, opportunities for productive friction multiply. Similarly, by requiring regular assessment of the progress of near-term operating and organizational initiatives relative to a longer-term destination, this approach to strategy encourages executives to look for patterns of impact among near-term initiatives and to propagate learning rapidly throughout relevant process networks. This approach in effect amplifies the opportunities for, and the impact of, productive friction throughout the organization.

REAPING THE REWARDS:
FROM INSIGHT TO INNOVATION

Deeper insight is valuable, but it is not the ultimate test for approaches to strategy development. Instead, the real question is whether the approach can generate meaningful, positive, and sustained improvements in performance for the firm. By enhancing organizational momentum and shaping institutional innovation, the approach just discussed becomes a powerful driver of performance improvement.

Overcoming Organizational Inertia

The approach to strategy outlined here and the performance fabrics described earlier help overcome organizational inertia by creating a platform for radical incrementalism. By radical incrementalism, we mean the ability to introduce at the local level radical changes that are still incremental relative to all the other elements of the business at the global level.[16] Implementing radical changes to business practices at the local level has typically been very difficult in more hardwired process environments. Performance fabrics enable radical change at the local level by strengthening the potential for loose coupling, both at the business level (as shared meaning and dynamic trust) and at the technology level (as distributed technology architectures). By supporting broadly distributed process networks, performance fabrics make it easier for any participant in these networks to implement radical changes within its own enterprise while minimizing the risk of disruptive effects across extended business processes.

Performance fabrics, however, can only create the capacity for change. New strategy approaches must harness that capacity by driving executives to design rapid waves of well-focused incremental business initiatives. Like DNA, these performance fabrics and strategic approaches will interweave to help companies overcome organizational inertia.

In particular, these fabrics and approaches will help address two traditional sources of organizational resistance—mind-set and culture—thereby transforming organizational DNA at an even more fundamental level. Mind-sets—the assumptions, often implicit, that executives bring to their decision making—often become a significant barrier to rapid change.[17] Most executives view uncertainty as a disruptive force, something to be avoided wherever possible. This is especially true when the organization falls into a reactive mode, with no clear view of longer-term direction, and is hampered by hardwired business or technology platforms. In a reactive environment, uncertainty creates additional demands on scarce resources and increases risk for existing initiatives. On the other hand, if the management team has a shared view of long-term direction, clearly identifying new opportunities created by uncertainty and change, executives begin to embrace uncertainty as a source of value creation.

These changing views of uncertainty also foster more openness to exploring the periphery as the most promising area for value creation. If uncertainty is something to be feared, then executives typically focus on internal operations of the business because they can manage uncertainty most effectively there. If uncertainty creates opportunity for additional value creation, then executives will venture beyond the boundaries of their enterprise or their industry, exploring new kinds of relationships with business partners or customers.[18]

They will also think more broadly about relevant markets and industries, seeking opportunities beyond the horizon of well-established (and well-understood) market niches.

The emphasis on near-term initiatives and results helps executives resist a mind-set favoring big-bang transformational initiatives. Instead, they focus on finding high-value, relatively easy-to-implement operational initiatives that can yield tangible, near-term business impact. By making these near-term initiatives easier to implement, performance fabrics contribute to the success of executives who focus on near-term results.

Radical incrementalism helps refashion organizational culture as well. By rewarding those who move most aggressively to seek near-term impact, this approach fosters a more risk-taking and performance-driven culture. It also encourages more willingness to leverage third-party resources to add value to customers in the near term. Executives are rewarded for performance delivered, rather than size of head count or assets managed. Greater clarity around long-term direction also makes it easier for executives to determine which resources a firm must own to realize long-term value and which third parties can provide complementary resources to enhance market impact.

Enhancing the Potential for
Institutional Innovation

The FAST strategy deepens and extends the innovation capabilities of enterprises. Forcing participants to confront difficult business issues across two parallel time horizons helps generate productive friction at both the top and the edge of the enterprise. Stressing the role of process networks as vehicles for deploying near-term operating initiatives helps expand the scope of specialized capabilities that can be mobilized to support near-term business innovations. Finally, the focus on performance fabrics helps reduce organizational inertia and accelerate deployment of near-term innovations as well as longer-term capability-building initiatives. It is this convergence of productive friction, process networks, and performance fabrics that defines the innovative power of the FAST strategy.

This approach will help generate and disseminate considerable product and process innovation. In the end, however, it will catalyze much more fundamental institutional innovation, redefining the boundaries and the role of the firm. In the process, the FAST approach will force us to revisit and reformulate some of the most basic principles of business and economic life. Adam Smith and David Ricardo introduced us to the virtues of specialization in work practices and comparative advantage across nations, but now we have opportunities for even higher levels of specialization at the level of the enterprise. With his insights about transaction costs and the relative efficiency of firms and markets in managing those costs, Ronald Coase helped define the rationale for the firm. We can now enrich the notion of transaction costs to focus more explicitly on the challenges of building capability. In the process, we will reconceive the firm as a vehicle for accelerated capability building—a firm that operates within broader process networks designed to amplify these capability-building efforts.

WHERE'S THE STRATEGIC ADVANTAGE?

In outlining this approach to strategy, we come full circle back to the beginning of this book. We live in a world of intensifying competition. Current approaches to strategy have clearly been inadequate. We argued that the contours of a new business strategy would effectively integrate three broad imperatives: focus tightly on distinctive internal capabilities, effectively mobilize the capabilities of other specialized business partners, and harness productive friction to accelerate capability building across networks of business partners. The book then sought to develop each of these imperatives in greater detail.

This new business strategy requires a very different approach. The FAST strategy is specifically designed to help senior management shift its focus from near-term efficiency improvements within the enterprise to longer-term capability building across process networks while at the same time delivering aggressive, near-term improvements in operating performance.

This approach assumes that we must redefine the notion of sustainable competitive advantage, but not in static terms. Instead, we must reconceive it as a trajectory of accelerated organizational capability building, guided by a long-term strategic direction. Rapid waves of operational initiatives, generating near-term innovations in work practices and performance improvement across process networks, provide the means for organizational capability building. The waves of near-term innovation and performance improvement cumulatively reshape the enterprise and the process networks within which it operates.

The institutional ability to shape and support continuing waves of operational innovation becomes the real source of sustainable competitive advantage because it creates distinctive organizational capability that cannot be copied. Organizational capability emerges from productive friction. It is deeply embedded in the shared understanding and shared practices that arise from addressing challenging business problems. For this reason, capability cannot simply be lifted out of one organizational context and implanted into other organizations. In other words, the organizational capability becomes *path dependent*—there is no easy way to leapfrog by copying the innovations of leaders in particular markets or industries.

By reconceiving strategic advantage as the dynamic evolution of organizational capability, this approach highlights the changing role of the corporation. As we have discussed, the rationale for the firm traditionally hinged on the ability to more efficiently manage interaction costs. This new strategy suggests that the rationale for the firm will increasingly focus on accelerating capability building. As we have emphasized throughout this book, the need for capability building does not stop at the border of the enterprise. In fact, companies that master the techniques required to accelerate capability building across broad networks of enterprises will be in the best position to generate superior returns. These companies will amplify the value of their own specialization by deepening the capabilities of their business partners.

These changes will not occur overnight. Certainly, big-bang efforts to transform the enterprise will generally fail. Companies must pursue pragmatic migration paths, building off current capabilities and focusing on near-term performance improvements. While specific migration paths will vary by company, we suggested that companies will generally evolve through three waves of capability building. In the first wave, companies will shift from their current focus on efficiency to a deeper focus on specialization and building distinctive capabilities. This leads to a second wave, in which companies realize that they must become more effective at mobilizing the resources and capabilities of other specialized enterprises to amplify the value of their own specialization. Finally, companies will confront a third wave of evolution as they recognize that coordinating the existing resources across enterprises is not sufficient—the real opportunity is to amplify value further by accelerating capability building across broad networks of business partners.

The good news is that these waves of change can be pursued incrementally, with tangible business value generated in each wave. The bad news is that there are no shortcuts. Because these changes are path dependent and specific to each enterprise, there is no easy way for laggards to catch up. Companies that fail to understand the changes required or that fail to move quickly along this migration path become vulnerable to more aggressive competitors. Your next business strategy is not an option; it is an imperative. And timing matters.

In this book, we have focused on the challenges and opportunities confronting enterprises. At the same time, we should recognize that the offshoring trends and the responses of enterprises will have much broader social and political effects. As we move from narrow wage arbitrage to much more sophisticated skill arbitrage within extended process networks, we can reshape opportunities for economic development on a global scale and redefine comparative advantage as distinctive skill sets shaped by specific cultural contexts and rapidly evolving and increasingly specialized local business ecosystems. Where value originates and who captures it will increasingly depend on the evolution of talent markets and the relative capability of firms (and nations) to rapidly develop and amplify the value of this talent. Product markets and financial markets will of course still matter, but the center of gravity for value creation and capture will inexorably migrate to global talent markets.

THE BOTTOM LINE

Members of senior management in most companies today generally view themselves as highly unified, well-functioning teams. But probe a little deeper, and you will often find that this sense of unity is maintained through conflict avoidance. What kind of company must we become? The future is too uncertain to hazard an answer. Which critical near-term initiatives will determine our success? We cannot rely on any one initiative, because of uncertainty, and so we will assemble a broad portfolio of initiatives and reassure ourselves that at least some of them will succeed. Do we have the right kind of organization to ensure success? Our organization will evolve naturally, adapting to changing circumstances. If we just keep our heads down and focus on responding to near-term events, we will evolve our way to success.

The approach we have outlined in this chapter penetrates this pseudo-unity by forcing senior executives to confront difficult questions regarding the future of their business. By creating the conditions for productive friction at the senior level of the company, this approach accelerates learning and helps align the entire organization.

Build alignment on the long-term direction of the company. As a member of the senior management team, you must build a shared view of where the company must head. This will not happen overnight, but it can be built through an ongoing process designed to answer the three questions highlighted earlier in this chapter:

- What will our relevant markets look like five to ten years from now?

- Which specialized capabilities should we distinctively own to generate the most value in these markets?

- Which process networks of complementary capability will be most effective in amplifying the value of our own distinctive specialization and in accelerating our capability building over time?

Structure this process as a series of senior management meetings, starting with a high degree of frequency (perhaps every two weeks) in the early stages and then tapering off to roughly every six weeks. Design early meetings to expand horizons and options, challenging conventional assumptions about the business. Bring in outside experts, especially from peripheral areas of the business, as a helpful way to expose senior executives to new perspectives. Visiting the periphery as a team is often essential to building shared insight. Scenario development can provide a structured way to explore alternative futures for the business. At the end of each session, identify the key uncertainties emerging from your discussion and assign working teams to gather data and develop perspectives on these uncertainties as preparation for the next meeting.

As these meetings progress, seek to develop preliminary answers for the three focusing questions, identifying key areas of disagreement and determining approaches that will help resolve these disagreements. As suggested earlier in this chapter, the challenge will be to answer these questions at a specific enough level that they can effectively guide difficult choices regarding near-term resource allocation while still remaining broad enough to avoid locking into a too-detailed view of the future. As your management team begins to converge around a shared view of the long-term direction, you should also identify key early indicators that will help validate or call into question this direction. Regularly review these early indicators, and discuss their implications for refinement (or, in extreme cases, abandonment) of the long-term direction.

To sustain a meaningful longer-term direction, explicitly identify what you will not do as a business. Most companies will probably shed broad areas of activities for which other firms have developed world-class capabilities.

Build alignment around near-term operating initiatives. In parallel, engage in a debate to build agreement around the two to three operating initiatives that over the next six to twelve months will be the most powerful in improving operating performance to the business. As noted, these discussions should explicitly include operating initiatives that extend beyond the boundaries of the enterprise and help build the performance of the broader process networks that will be important for delivering more value to customers.

This debate will usually surface differences in key assumptions about the future of the business. These differences will be helpful in framing the discussions around long-term direction. As you begin to agree on the two to three near-term operating initiatives, also seek to build agreement on two other issues:

- What are appropriate yet aggressive operating performance objectives that can be achieved in a six- to twelve-month time frame?

- What is the critical mass of resources (in all dimensions—financial, technological, and human—across all relevant enterprises) that will ensure the success of these operating initiatives?

These discussions in turn will probably surface the underlying reality—resources are scarce. Helping to ensure the success of the highest-priority operating initiatives will likely require scaling back other initiatives and eliminating many others altogether. This in turn will force you to revisit priorities and make sure that they are really focused on the highest-impact initiatives. It will also force difficult choices regarding specialization that feed back into the discussions around longer-term direction.

Identify and address major organizational barriers. As you engage in discussions on critical near-term operating initiatives, explicitly ask what is preventing the organization from moving even more quickly to achieve higher levels of performance in these areas. In parallel, identify two to three organizational initiatives that can have meaningful impact over the next six to twelve months in breaking down the barriers that prevent even more aggressive operational movement.

Create tight performance feedback loops. To maximize learning from these parallel efforts, also review on a regular basis key performance metrics from these operating and organizational initiatives. This performance feedback will help refine efforts along all three dimensions—definition of longer-term direction, deployment of aggressive near-term operating initiatives, and implementation of targeted organizational initiatives.

Epilogue

Recasting Public Policy to Develop Talent

W
e have written a book for business executives regarding business strategy, not a book on public policy. Nor do we presume to set a public policy agenda here. Nevertheless, our perspective on business strategy does have important implications for public policy.

At the end of the book, we implied that value creation will increasingly focus on talent markets, rather than product markets or financial markets. These markets will continue to generate enormous value, but the evolution of talent markets will shape their dynamics. A company's ability—indeed, a country's ability—to attract, retain, and develop talent, rather than exploit natural resources, will define comparative advantage for the enterprise or the region. So, on a macro-economic level, comparative advantage becomes more dynamic: where natural resources are largely fixed (and generally depleting), talent can grow and create opportunities for more rapid shifts in relative position, because of its susceptibility to increasing returns dynamics.

In the past century, policy makers have generally crafted economic agendas around overarching goals defined as natural resource development, industrial development, or development of robust financial markets. We suggest that economic policy agendas of the twenty-first century must focus instead much more aggressively on talent development. Development of other resources and markets will of course continue to be important. But the value of these resources and markets will increasingly be shaped by the relative success in building comparative advantage in talent markets. By looking at the broad range of public policy through the lens of talent development, many seemingly unrelated public policies can be reconceived at a fundamental level and brought together in ways that will reinforce their impact.

In hearing us talk about talent development, many readers will likely think we are focusing on educational policy. Far from it. While educational policy will certainly play a role as a starting point in building comparative advantage in talent markets, we believe it will play a far smaller role than most people imagine. There is no doubt a significant risk that policy makers will become so focused on educational policy that they will lose sight of the much broader ways that public policy can shape talent development.

Prepare talent more effectively. Educational policy usually fixates on the formal institutions that prepare individuals for productive participation in the marketplace and civil society—more broadly, elementary and secondary schools and colleges and universities. These institutions have been shaped by a mind-set—students proceed through a largely standardized track of educational programs at specified periods in their life to become prepared for life experiences. The learning required for talent development generally requires a much broader array of informal mechanisms extending over an individual's lifetime and shaped by a mind-set—mobilizing resources and shaping experiences as required by the individual at a time of perceived need, rather than as determined in a top-down manner by policy makers and standardized tests.

Nevertheless, formal educational institutions will continue to play a role in a broader effort to develop talent. Public policy must strengthen these core educational institutions by fostering more performance-driven institutional innovation. Just as enterprises must accelerate their own capability building, educational institutions must focus on more rapidly enhancing their own core capabilities. Institutions of learning must transform themselves into learning institutions, continually reflecting on, and seeking to improve, the performance of their processes. In part, public policy can encourage this transformation by creating more opportunities for local (and, especially at the college and university level, global) competition and experimentation.

We expect that this competition and experimentation will help shift the institutional mind-set from push to pull. Several beneficial effects are likely. As educational institutions become more responsive to the needs of their students, the schools are likely in many parts of the world to shift from an emphasis on rote memorization to fostering the ability to think critically and to appropriate knowledge in ways that serve the needs of the individual and evolving work environments. The institutions must prepare students to become reflective practitioners who pursue lifelong learning with passion, helping them participate more effectively in the networked and dynamic global economy.

More generally, as mind-sets shift, institutions of higher education are likely to extend their horizons, both in addressing the lifelong needs of learning, rather than focusing on narrow slices of a student's life, and in developing more versatile ways of engaging students. Rather than requiring students to come together at a central location for all their educational experiences, educational institutions will begin to develop more flexible, hybrid forms of distance learning and on-site learning. Learning institutions are bringing together groups of students in dispersed locations, as pioneered by institutions like the University of Phoenix in the United States and the Open University of England. These innovative approaches are also creating more flexibility for students to pursue education while working at the same time.

Remove barriers to movement to pull talent into more rewarding development opportunities. But, as we have said, formal education is a relatively small part of the overall public policy challenge in developing talent. If talent is to develop fully, policy makers must focus on removing barriers to the movement of talent, across both geographic and enterprise borders. Talent will only develop fully if deployed against the areas of greatest opportunity and greatest value. Talent cannot develop in isolation—it requires a rich set of experiences and interactions to fully blossom. This policy approach fostering freer movement may be particularly difficult for policy makers concerned about brain drain—the instinct is to hold on to talent, rather than acknowledge that others have been more successful in creating opportunities for talent utilization and development. Surprisingly, the freer movement of talent provides a compelling performance feedback mechanism for measuring the ability to attract, retain, and develop talent.

This approach applies at both a geographic level as immigration (and emigration) policy and an enterprise level as employment protection laws. Many countries, most notably the United States, have benefited from the immigration of talent. As one often-overlooked example, the fertile innovation of Silicon Valley depended at least in part on its ability to attract extremely talented engineers from India and China. Of course, India and China were concerned about the departure of these young engineers. And yet, talented engineers returning from Silicon Valley to places like Bangalore, Taipei, and Shenzhen are fueling much of the dynamic entrepreneurial spirit that characterizes these areas today.

If public policy inhibits the movement of talent from one enterprise to another, it will lock in individuals to situations that will not fully challenge them and that will not generate more value for them or for their enterprises. Developing talent requires a rich interaction of theory and practice. Theory—a sense of knowing what and why—shapes, and is in turn shaped by, practice, a sense of knowing how. Talent cannot develop without practice, and the most powerful forms of practice require sustained interaction with others. Only by interacting closely with others can talent access the powerful local knowledge that is required for the enrichment and advancement of its practice. If talent is locked into enterprises that are failing to generate value, its development will be severely constrained—it will remain embedded in low-value environments that cannot maximize the value of the talent available or provide it with the incentives and opportunity to develop more fully. Individuals with talent may seek to remain in these enterprises because of inertia, but broader market forces can provide the stimulus to redeploy this talent into more challenging and rewarding environments.

Freer labor markets help increase the bargaining power of talent by demanding more effective development platforms. Enhanced labor mobility makes it easier for innovative companies to attract the best and brightest, not only with higher salaries but also with more rapid opportunities for the use of existing talent and for the further development of that talent. Conversely, less innovative companies are penalized as they lose their talent—the result is a powerful performance feedback loop that forces changes in practices. By removing barriers to labor mobility, public policy can enhance the ability to pull talent into the most rewarding and challenging opportunities, thereby accelerating the development of talent within and across enterprises. It is no accident that in Silicon Valley, where job mobility is extremely high, CEOs of successful companies often had surprisingly undistinguished college careers, if they went to college at all. Silicon Valley itself provides a rich learning culture and array of learning experiences for the rapid development of talent.

Expand opportunities for talent development. Productive friction is an important catalyst for talent development. To enhance the potential for productive friction, policy makers must encourage the exposure of local people and businesses to as many flows as possible—flows of people, products, financial capital, and ideas.

We have already discussed the importance of labor mobility in enabling talent to access the most rewarding and challenging opportunities. Labor mobility plays another important role in enhancing cross-pollination and rejuvenating existing talent. As people move from one enterprise to another or one geographical location to another, they bring with them a new set of perspectives, practices, ideas, and experiences that can spur innovation.

Similarly, freer flows of products and services across geographic boundaries also create the potential for productive friction. By having to compete with a more diverse array of products and services, local talent is forced to develop more innovative approaches to the marketplace. By having more choices available to them, customers can become important sources of productive friction, richly rewarding companies that successfully serve their evolving needs while increasing penalties for those that fall short in serving these needs.

Flows of investment capital can also accelerate talent development. For example, the early investments of multinational companies like Texas Instruments and General Electric helped attract and develop talent in Bangalore in the 1980s and 1990s. Similarly, investments by Taiwanese companies are playing a similar role in accelerating the development of specialized electronics ecosystems in coastal regions of China.

Communications and transportation infrastructures are essential to the expansion of these flows over time. For instance, the more rapid modernization of shipping ports in China explains at least in part why there is a faster growth in trade flows between the United States and China than between the United States and India.

Broadband communication networks will play an especially critical role in enhancing the potential for productive friction across borders. Much of the discussion on broadband networks focuses on consumer markets, but the role of these networks in business-to-business markets has often been mostly overlooked (ironically, especially in many of the more developed economies). These networks will be essential to support the deployment of service-oriented architectures as well as much lower-cost voice- and video-over IP and the next generation of social software. As we have seen, these technologies will be key enablers of productive friction across enterprise and geographic boundaries.

Broadband networks will also facilitate access to powerful distributed tools for problem solving like the robotic telescopes located in Hawaii and Australia in the Faulkes Telescope Project. Students in distant locations pursuing science projects can control these telescopes remotely. High-resolution images are transmitted back to the users in real time. Countries adopting policies promoting the rapid deployment of broadband networks will undoubtedly foster the innovation potential of their economies and thereby accelerate the potential for more rapid (and more dispersed) talent development. Wireless networks are likely to play a similar role in supporting talent development, enhancing the ability of people to connect more readily with other people and necessary resources, wherever both might be located.

Foster incentives for the more rapid development of talent. Many public policy agendas focus on push incentives for the development of talent—agencies identify promising talent arenas and then design targeted subsidies to develop talent. We would suggest that pull incentives, as the freer movement of investment funds and more stable legal infrastructures, are likely to be much more effective in enabling talent to find its highest value outlets and in creating more effective mechanisms for sustained and rapid development of that talent.

Robust venture-capital markets can help talent break out of conventional business environments and pursue innovations along multiple dimensions—technology, product, process, practice, and business models—in much less constrained greenfield environments. In addition to cash, venture capitalists provide significant mentoring of entrepreneurs and access to broader networks of business relationships that can be very helpful in accelerating growth. Well-developed public debt and equity markets can help accelerate the growth of successful innovations, providing opportunities for the rapid development of talent in more innovative ventures. Private equity markets, on the other hand, provide a mechanism for the restructuring of operations and businesses through leveraged buyouts to create more promising talent-development platforms. Well-developed financial markets in general provide a mechanism for redeploying capital away from less promising talent-development platforms to more attractive ones.

In parallel, the rule of law and especially the consistent and efficient enforcement of property and contract law help create incentives for the longer-term development of talent. In countries whose laws are arbitrarily enforced or whose legal remedies are extremely time-consuming or expensive to access, individuals and enterprises typically adopt much shorter time horizons, requiring quick payback. The talent that flourishes in these environments is the talent of the quick deal, not the talent that patiently nurtures innovations over the long term. Incremental innovations may still be feasible in these environments, but breakthrough innovations are less likely.

This emphasis on the rule of law is different from a perspective that insists on uniformity of laws across national boundaries. If we are to foster more robust flows across national boundaries, we must learn to honor and cope with an increasingly heterogeneous world. After all, one of the greatest opportunities for productive friction may reside at the level of public policy. Different legal and public policy regimes can effectively compete to attract, retain, and develop talent. This opportunity also exists within national boundaries. One key to the recent growth of both the Indian and the Chinese economies has been the experimentation in public policy and competition emerging across states and provinces, respectively, within these countries.

In the legal arena, one of the most contentious public policy issues involves approaches to the enforcement of intellectual property rights. More-developed economies, especially the United States, have moved over time to policies that heavily protect existing owners of intellectual property. Remarkably, the United States, in its earlier history, was much more tolerant of the "borrowing" of intellectual property from others, as witnessed by the frequent protests from British companies that their ideas were being appropriated without adequate compensation. Developing economies often worry less about protecting the rights of the existing owners of intellectual property and more about ensuring broader access to intellectual property. Either extreme usually dampens incentives for innovation. If innovators cannot reap adequate rewards for their creations, they will be less likely to invest the time and effort required to discover new approaches, especially if significant investments and lead times are involved. On the other hand, if the next generation of innovators finds its access to previous intellectual property blocked by prohibitive fees or barriers, these innovators will be significantly hampered in building on the accomplishments of the past. To accelerate the development of talent, policy makers must strike an effective balance between these two extremes of intellectual property protection.

Again, we must learn to honor heterogeneity in this sphere as well, recognizing that no single intellectual property regime is likely to be right, since the regimes serve the interests of different countries at different points in time. By creating the potential for productive friction in this sphere, we may discover innovative approaches to striking an appropriate balance between diverse interests.

Reduce disincentives for developing talent. Talent will not develop rapidly if paralyzed by fear of failure. Talent cannot develop without exploration and experimentation, yet these activities inevitably create significant risk of failure. If failure is not recognized and even celebrated, people and enterprises are much less likely to take risks in the first place or to learn from failure after it occurs. Public policy can play a significant role in shaping both the perceived risk of failure and the ability to rapidly adjust and learn from it.

Bankruptcy laws can ease the recovery from failures, especially in launching new businesses. In countries in which these laws are too stringent, talent may hesitate to launch the ventures that could provide significant learning potential and may instead remain ensconced in more traditional business settings, potentially limiting any development potential. Of course, as with intellectual property law, if bankruptcy laws heavily favor debtors, then investors may not invest in risky ventures, limiting the availability of financing for talent with creative new business ideas.

In many countries around the world, talent remains embedded in low-growth, poorly performing businesses because public policy seeks to prop up failing enterprises. Usually this occurs when the banking system is discouraged from writing off bad loans and public policy helps banks generate additional credit to be funneled into these failing enterprises. By encouraging banks to clean up their balance sheets, public policy can make it easier for banks to acknowledge bad loans and to divert credit to more promising enterprises. This in turn will encourage talent embedded in these companies to seek employment in enterprises that could offer much more attractive development potential.

At the end of the day, the most painful consequences of failure are felt at the level of the individual worker, especially workers who possess outmoded skills. Thrown out of jobs that they may have held for decades, these workers not only can feel near-term financial pressure, but also frequently endure the long and painful process of finding alternative work, often at much lower salary levels than before. Again, public policy can play a role in helping to ease these transitions significantly. Working with companies to increase the portability of health care programs and pension plans, as the McKinsey Global Institute has suggested, could substantially reduce the financial penalties incurred by workers as they move from one company to another. Similarly, the Brookings Institution has developed an insurance proposal to help workers displaced by trade in manufactures. Tax credits and other incentives can also encourage companies to provide retraining for workers. Pull-oriented programs, in which the companies hiring displaced workers provide the training, are likely to work more effectively than push-oriented programs, which require governments to anticipate which skills are likely to be most valuable. Public policy designed to remove obstacles to the transition of workers from poorly performing enterprises to more promising companies can play a material role in accelerating talent development within the economy.

We have avoided proposing specific public policies, preferring instead to briefly outline some broad principles for public policy formation. These principles stem from our overarching view that public policy agendas must be reoriented around the broader goal of accelerating talent development. As with business strategy, specific public policies must provide long-term views of destination and unique starting points.

Nevertheless, we believe that a fundamental shift in perspective will help public policies become more effective. At one level, the perspective of policy makers needs to shift from a relatively static view of the world to a much more dynamic one. Talent development is an inherently dynamic and cumulative process—it requires an understanding of potential trajectories and path dependencies. Each wave of talent development creates new possibilities and new wealth for society. Static views of the world quickly turn opportunities for productive friction and further talent development into threats of destructive friction that can spiral rapidly out of control. If resources are fixed, then the battle lines form around the distribution of resources, rather than bringing people together around the opportunity to expand resources through talent development.

The perspective of policy makers also needs to shift from conventional, push views of government policy, in which the needs are determined in advance, usually from the top down, and investments made to address these needs. Instead, policy makers should explore more pull-oriented approaches to public policy—removing barriers to the movement of people and resources and creating appropriate incentives for talent to seek out what it needs to develop more fully.

These two shifts in perspective—from static to dynamic and from push to pull—are related. Push-oriented public policies might be more feasible in static environments, when needs might be anticipated more effectively. As environments become more dynamic and unpredictable, push approaches begin to fall apart. In their place, pull-oriented policies can help ensure that appropriate resources are available when needed, even though those needs cannot be readily anticipated, especially in talent development. When faced with a particular challenge or opportunity, we are much more motivated to learn new approaches and integrate them effectively into our conceptual models and practices.

By focusing on talent development, policy makers can help individuals in their society more effectively realize their full potential. But the benefits extend far beyond this. Talent development, especially when situated in economic activity, can drive improved productivity and, in turn, enhance the standard of living in any society. Even more broadly, a focus on talent development helps attract highly motivated and creative people and provides them with the resources and time to develop a rich and evolving cultural and social environment. Talent development is an ongoing race, but those who lead the race will unleash passion and rewards that will make the race worth running.

Notes

Chapter 1

1. "What Doth It Profit?" *Economist,* December 6, 2001, 65; and "A Survey of the World Economy," *Economist,* 28 September 2002, 9.

2. Richard Foster and Sarah Kaplan, *Creative Destruction: Why Companies That Are Built to Last Underperform the Market—and How to Successfully Transform Them* (New York: Currency Doubleday, 2001), 12–13.

3. McKinsey & Company conducted one of the most rigorous and broad-based efforts to quantify the impact of interaction costs on business activity around the world. The results of this effort were summarized in Patrick Butler et al., "A Revolution in Interaction," *McKinsey Quarterly,* no. 1 (1997): 4–23. In its study, McKinsey used the term *interaction costs* rather than *transaction costs* to emphasize that the activities involved more than the costs of exchanging items of value, but also included the costs of searching, coordinating, and monitoring work. More traditionally, economists have used the term *transaction costs* broadly to capture these activities, as in Ronald Coase, "The Nature of the Firm," *Economica* 4, no. 16 (1937): 386–405.

4. A broad overview of these public policy shifts on a global scale is available in Daniel Yergin and Joseph Stanislaw, *The Commanding Heights: The Battle Between Government and the Marketplace That Is Remaking the Modern World* (New York: Simon & Schuster, 1998). Lowell Bryan and Diana Farrell provide an interesting perspective on the public policy shifts and corresponding market developments that have led to the emergence of truly global financial markets, in *Market Unbound: Unleashing Global Capitalism* (New York: John Wiley & Sons, 1996). Another interesting perspective on the deregulation of financial markets is provided by Raghuram G. Rajan and Luigi Zingales, *Saving Capitalism from the Capitalists: Unleashing the Power of Financial Markets to Create Wealth and Spread Opportunity* (New York: Crown Business, 2003).

5. For example, the removal of trade quotas in apparel in 2005 will likely have a significant impact on the geographic distribution of apparel production.

6. The concept of reverse markets is developed more fully in John Hagel III and Marc Singer, "Reverse Markets," in *Net Worth: The Emerging Role of the Infomediary in the Race for Customer Information* (Boston: Harvard Business School Press, 1999), chap. 10. For a more recent exploration of the business implications of more powerful customers, see C. K. Prahalad and Venkat Ramaswamy, *The Future of Competition: Co-Creating Unique Value with Customers* (Boston: Harvard Business School Press, 2004).

7. Lewis Carroll, *Through the Looking-Glass: And What Alice Found There* (New York: Dover, 1999). The growing prominence of this metaphor in the business world stems from a well-known principle in evolutionary biology known as the Red Queen Hypothesis, originally articulated by the paleontologist Lee Van Valen, of the University of Chicago, in "A New Evolutionary Theory," *Evolutionary Theory* 1 (1973): 1–30. In evolutionary biology, this hypothesis suggests that species must continue to evolve to avoid extinction.

8. Gary Hamel and C. K. Prahalad, *Competing for the Future: Breakthrough Strategies for Seizing Control of Your Industry and Creating the Markets of Tomorrow* (Boston: Harvard Business School Press, 1994).

9. Edith Penrose, *The Theory of the Growth of the Firm* (Oxford: Oxford University Press, 1959). Other notable works in the resource-based theory of the firm include B. Wernerfelt, "A Resource Based View of the Firm," *Strategic Management Journal* 5 (1984): 171–180; R. P. Rumelt, "Towards a Strategic Theory of the Firm," in *Competitive Strategic Management,* ed. R. B. Lamb (Englewood Cliff, NJ: Prentice Hall, 1984), 556–570; and J. B. Barney, "Firm Resources and Sustained Competitive Advantage," *Journal of Management* 17, no. 1 (1991): 99–120.

10. Adam M. Brandenburger and Barry J. Nalebuff, *Co-opetition* (New York: Currency Doubleday, 1996); and James F. Moore, *The Death of Competition: Leadership and Strategy in the Age of Business Ecosystems* (New York: Harper Business, 1996). See also Benjamin Gomes-Casseres, *The Alliance Revolution: The New Shape of Business Rivalry* (Cambridge, MA: Harvard University Press, 1996). There is a vast literature on the value of collaboration across enterprises. Unfortunately, most of the literature either focuses narrowly on bilateral relationships like strategic alliances or joint ventures or it goes to the other extreme of embracing all conceivable relationships across enterprises under relatively nebulous terms like networks or ecosystems. A good overview of this literature is available in David Faulkner and Mark De Rond, eds., *Cooperative Strategy: Economic, Business and Organizational Issues* (New York: Oxford University Press, 2000). We will cite some of the more helpful literature on business collaboration in chapters 2 and 4.

11. Business executives in particular have embraced the core-versus-context distinction popularized by Geoffrey A. Moore, *Living on the Fault Line: Managing for Shareholder Value in the Age of the Internet* (New York: Harper, 2000).

12. In our categorization of intangible resources, we are indebted to Lowell Bryan, Jane Fraser, Jeremy Oppenheim, and Wilhelm Rall, *Race for the World: Strategies to Build a Great Global Firm* (Boston: Harvard Business School Press, 1999).

13. In this context, we would cite the work of George Stalk and Thomas Hout, *Competing Against Time: How Time-Based Competition Is Reshaping Global Markets* (New York: Free Press, 1990). Stalk and Hout focus on a set of practices and processes designed to reduce cycle times in the delivery of value to the market, but if the result is to become a capability, these practices and processes must be coupled with specific resources to deliver distinctive value to the market. Otherwise, companies run the risk of falling into the dot-com trap of embracing speed, rather than distinctive value. See also George Stalk, Philip Evans, and Lawrence E. Shulman, "Competing on Capabilities: The New Rules of Corporate Strategy," *Harvard Business Review* (March–April 1992) 57–69.

14. A rich strategy literature highlights the importance of dynamic capability building within the firm, starting, most notably, with Joseph A. Schumpeter, *Capitalism, Socialism and Democracy* (New York: Harper, 1942); Richard M. Cyert and James G. March, *A Behavioral Theory of the Firm* (Englewood Cliffs, NJ: Prentice Hall, 1963); and Richard Nelson and Sydney Winter, *An Evolutionary Theory of Economic Change* (Cambridge, MA: Belknap Press, 1982); but then further developed by Robert Hayes, Steven Wheelwright, and Kim Clark, *Dynamic Manufacturing: Creating the Learning Organization* (New York: Free Press, 1988); and Peter M. Senge, *The Fifth Discipline: The Art and Practice of the Learning Organization* (New York: Currency Doubleday, 1990). See also Bruce Kogut and Udo Zander, "Knowledge of the Firm and the Evolutionary Theory of the Multinational Corporation," *Journal of International Business Studies* 24, no. 4 (1993): 625–645; Ikujiro Nonaka and Hirotaka Takeuchi, *The Knowledge-Creating Company* (New York: Oxford University Press, 1995); and D. Teece, G. Pisano, and A. Shuen, "Dynamic Capabilities and Strategic Management," *Strategic Management Journal* 18, no. 7 (1997): 509–533. For a related perspective on dynamic transaction costs, see Richard N. Langlois and Paul L. Robertson, *Firms, Markets and Economic Change: A Dynamic Theory of Business Institutions* (New York: Routledge, 1995). With rare exceptions, however, these perspectives remain very enterprise-centric, focused on the challenge and mechanisms of building capability within the firm, rather than systematically looking at

opportunities to accelerate capability building through relationships with other firms. Even Shona L. Brown and Kathleen M. Eisenhardt, in their excellent book *Competing on the Edge: Strategy as Structured Chaos* (Boston: Harvard Business School Press, 1998), end up focusing on multiple business units within a single enterprise in their discussion of coadaptation, rather than emphasizing the opportunity to apply this technique across enterprises.

15. See, in addition to the sources cited in the previous footnote, K. M. Eisenhardt and J. Martin, "Dynamic Capabilities: What Are They?" *Strategic Management Journal* 21 (2000): 1105–1121; and Sidney G. Winter, "Understanding Dynamic Capabilities," working paper, Reginald H. Jones Center, The Wharton School, University of Pennsylvania, Philadelphia, 2002.

16. Henry Chesbrough, *Open Innovation: The New Imperative for Creating and Profiting from Technology* (Boston: Harvard Business School Press, 2003).

17. In an e-mail to the authors on September 28, 2004, Bill Joy indicated that he made this statement many times in speeches throughout the 1980s.

18. Coase, "The Nature of the Firm." Business and strategy literature largely ignored this essay until Oliver Williamson revived it, most notably in *Markets and Hierarchies* (New York: Free Press, 1975). Building on Coase, Williamson spawned a rich literature on the role of transaction cost economics in shaping the boundaries of the firm. See Christos Pitelis, ed., *Transaction Costs, Markets and Hierarchies* (Oxford: Basil Blackwell, 1993); A. Madhok, "The Organization of Economic Activity: Transaction Costs, Firm Capabilities and the Nature of Governance," *Organization Science* 7 (1996): 577–590; and M. Maher, "Transaction Cost Economics and Contractual Relations," *Cambridge Journal of Economics* 21 (1997): 147–170.

19. Alfred D. Chandler Jr., *Strategy and Structure: Chapters in the History of the American Industrial Enterprise* (Cambridge, MA: MIT Press, 1962). Although Chandler's work is often cited to support the transaction cost theory of the firm, Chandler himself declared strong sympathies with the evolutionary capabilities school. See Alfred D. Chandler Jr., "Organizational Capabilities and the Economic History of the Industrial Enterprise," *Journal of Economic Perspectives* 6 (summer 1992): 79–100.

20. For key analytic tools required to construct this new rationale for the firm, see John Seely Brown and Paul Duguid, *The Social Life of Information* (Boston: Harvard Business School Press, 2000); and David Teece, "Profiting from Technological Innovation: Implications for Integration, Collaboration, Licensing, and Public Policy," *Research Policy* 15 (1986): 285–305.

21. Brian Loasby, *Knowledge, Institutions and Evolution in Economics* (London: Routledge, 1999); and Alfred Marshall, *Principles of Economics* (London: MacMillan, 1920). See also G. B. Richardson, *Information and Investment:*

A Study in the Working of the Competitive Economy (Oxford: Oxford University Press, 1960); G. B. Richardson, "The Organization of Industry," *Economic Journal* 82 (September 1972): 883–896; and the essay by Nicolai J. Foss, "Austrian and Post-Marshallian Economics: The Bridging Work of George Richardson" in *Economic Organization, Capabilities and Co-ordination*, ed. Nicolai J. Foss and Brian J. Loasby (London: Routledge, 1998). Friedrich A. Hayek, in his influential essays "Economics and Knowledge" (1937) and "The Use of Knowledge in Society" (1945), both re-published in Friedrich A. Hayek, *Individualism and Economic Order* (Chicago, University of Chicago Press, 1946), provided an insightful view of the role of knowledge in economic activity that remains a rich resource for those seeking to construct an alternative theory of the firm. This perspective on the shifting rationale for the firm is consistent with the dynamic capabilities literature cited in note 14.

22. William Gibson, *London Sunday Express*, March 29, 2000.

Chapter 2

1. The material in this chapter and chapter 3 benefited greatly from collaboration with John-Paul Ho, managing director of Crimson, and his colleagues, both at Crimson and at its portfolio companies.

2. Michael Dell, conversation with authors, May 21, 2003.

3. Derek Holley, president, eTelecare, interview with authors, December 10, 2003.

4. Interview with former executive of a global electronics manufacturing outsourcing company, January 3, 2004.

5. Ian Morton, partner, Crimson (a private equity firm in Palo Alto, CA, specializing in offshoring-related investments), interview with authors, December 23, 2003.

6. Cliff Chen, partner, Crimson, interview with authors, January 19, 2004.

7. Kris Gopalakrishnan, cofounder, deputy managing director, and chief operating officer, Infosys, interview with authors, June 19, 2004.

8. Ajay Gandhi, principal, Crimson, interview with authors, December 5, 2003.

9. Ibid.

10. Ashish Thadhani, "Secular Mega-Trends: India—The Software Outsourcing Superpower," *Brean Murray Research,* June 16, 2003. The Capability Maturity Model was originally developed at Carnegie Mellon University and defines five stages of process maturity in software development.

11. Chen, interview with authors.

12. For example, Jim Breyer, managing partner of Accel Partners and a leading venture capitalist in Silicon Valley, said, "Taiwan and China have some

of the world's best designers of wireless chips and wireless software." Jim Breyer, quoted in "No Smooth Sailing for Offshoring," *San Francisco Chronicle,* November 16, 2003.

13. John-Paul Ho, managing director, Crimson, interview with authors, December 11, 2003.

14. Ibid.

15. Ibid. For a broader discussion of the role of personal relationships in Chinese businesses, see Thomas Menkhoff and Solvay Gerke, eds., *Chinese Entrepreneurship and Asian Business Networks* (New York: Routledge, 2002).

16. Chen, interview with authors.

17. Holley, interview with authors.

18. Ibid.

19. Ibid.

20. Ibid.

21. Interview with former executive of a global electronics manufacturing outsourcing company, January 3, 2004.

22. Holley, interview with authors.

23. Chen, interview with authors.

24. Ho, interview with authors.

25. Information on this Taiwanese company in this section came from Chen, interview with authors.

26. Ho, interview with authors.

27. Discussions of many of these emerging specialized ecosystems in Asia can be found in Martin Kenney and Richard Florida, eds., *Locating Global Advantage: Industry Dynamics in the International Economy* (Palo Alto, CA: Stanford University Press, 2004). See also the more specialized works by David G. McKendrick, Richard F. Doner, and Stephan Haggard, *From Silicon Valley to Singapore: Location and Competitive Advantage in the Hard Disk Drive Industry* (Palo Alto, CA: Stanford University Press, 2000); and Thomas P. Murtha, Stefanie Ann Lenway, and Jeffrey A. Hart, *Managing New Industry Creation: Global Knowledge Formation and Entrepreneurship in High Technology* (Palo Alto, CA: Stanford University Press, 2001).

28. An interesting discussion of the role of public policy in fostering diverse specialized business ecosystems in China can be found in Adam Segal, *Digital Dragon: High Technology Enterprises in China* (Ithaca, NY: Cornell University Press, 2003).

29. For a discussion of the role of business ecosystems in sharing knowledge across enterprises, see John Seely Brown and Paul Duguid, "Mysteries of the Region: Knowledge Dynamics in Silicon Valley," in *The Silicon Valley Edge: A Habitat for Innovation and Entrepreneurship,* ed. Chong-Moon Lee et al. (Palo Alto,

CA: Stanford University Press, 2000). The economist Alfred Marshall drew attention to the economic importance of localization, in *Principles of Economics* (London: MacMillan and Co., 1890). Other more recent studies of the importance of business ecosystems include Jane Jacobs, *The Economy of Cities* (New York: Vintage, 1970); Annalee Saxenian, *Regional Advantage: Culture and Competition in Silicon Valley and Route 128* (Cambridge, MA: Harvard University Press, 1994); W. Brian Arthur, *Increasing Returns and Path Dependence in the Economy* (Ann Arbor: University of Michigan Press, 1994); Manuel Castells and Peter Hall, *Technopoles of the World: The Making of Twenty-First Century Industrial Complexes* (London: Routledge, 1994); Michael Porter, *The Competitive Advantage of Nations* (New York: Free Press, 1990); Michael Porter, "Clusters and the New Economics of Competition," *Harvard Business Review* (November–December 1998): 77–90; and Martin Kenney, ed., *Understanding Silicon Valley: The Anatomy of an Entrepreneurial Region* (Palo Alto, CA: Stanford University Press, 2000). Michael Porter's concept of clusters is far broader than our notion of local business ecosystems—he includes entire countries and even regions within a single cluster while we believe tighter geographic concentrations are necessary to really harness the opportunities for knowledge sharing across enterprises.

30. A good overview of the emergence and development of the specialized business ecosystem in Bangalore can be found in James Heitzman, *Network City: Planning the Information Society in Bangalore* (New York: Oxford University Press, 2004).

31. Vivek Kulkarni, chairman and CEO, B2K Corporation, interview with authors, June 17, 2004.

32. China IT Services Forum, conference in Santa Clara, California, sponsored by Focus Ventures, a venture capital firm, on June 5, 2004.

33. "Offshore Storm: The Global Razor's Edge," *Fast Company,* February 2004.

34. Kulkarni, interview with authors.

Chapter 3

1. Most of the vast strategy literature on the relationship between strategy and business focus often defines *focus* in terms of product or market businesses, particularly in a broader corporate portfolio. The classic work in this field, Richard Rumelt, *Strategy Structure and Economic Performance* (Cambridge, MA: Harvard University Press, 1974), finds that related diversification produced superior financial performance compared with unrelated diversification. For a useful overview of *business scope,* see Robert M. Grant, "Corporate Strategy: Managing Scope and Strategy Content," *Handbook of Strategy and Management,* ed. Andrew Pettigrew, Howard Thomas, and Richard Whittington (London: Sage 2002).

2. We are indebted to Eric Beinhocker, executive director, Corporate Executive Board, for pointing out that the last major buggy whip manufacturer—U.S. Whip Company—leveraged its expertise in braiding to evolve into a worldwide supplier of sport fishing lines, eventually changing its name to U.S. Line Company. It has continually adapted its braiding expertise to new synthetic fibers like nylon and Dacron, providing an interesting example of dynamic specialization. For more information, see the company's Web site, http://www.usline.com/About_Us/about_us.html.

3. This perspective continues to build on the core-competency and dynamic-capabilities schools of strategies cited in chapter 1 (see especially notes 8, 9, and 14), but argues more explicitly that companies need to shed nondifferentiating capabilities. For example, in *Competing for the Future* (Boston: Harvard Business School Press, 1994), Gary Hamel and C. K. Prahalad barely mention outsourcing or divestiture, much less feature them as major strategic initiatives to restructure the enterprise.

4. A provocative study by Boston Consulting Group found that many of the top-performing companies today began by scaling back and focusing their businesses more tightly before achieving high growth rates. See Daniel Stelter et al., *The Value Creators: A Study of the World's Top Performers* (Boston: Boston Consulting Group, 1999).

5. Vivek Paul, vice chairman and president, Wipro Technologies, interview with authors, June 2, 2004; Sambuddha Deb, chief quality officer, Wipro Technologies, interview with authors, July 22, 2004; and Kris Gopalakrishnan, cofounder, deputy managing director, and chief operating officer, Infosys, interview with authors, June 19, 2004.

6. For a fuller development of these three business types and the rationale for focusing on only one type, see John Hagel and Marc Singer, "Unbundling the Corporation," *Harvard Business Review* (March–April 1999): 133–141; and John Hagel, *Out of the Box: Strategies for Achieving Profits Today and Growth Tomorrow* (Boston: Harvard Business School Press, 2002), chap. 7. Other writers have recently argued for specialization but with different meanings. For example, in *Profit from the Core: Growth Strategy in an Era of Turbulence* (Boston: Harvard Business School Press, 2001), Chris Zook and James Allen maintain that companies should focus on their "core business," but define *core* more broadly than our three business types. In *The Discipline of Market Leaders: Choose Your Customers, Narrow Your Focus and Dominate Your Market* (Reading, MA: Addison-Wesley, 1995), Michael Treacy and Fred Wiersema argue that companies should build their organization around a single "value discipline" (which roughly corresponds to the three business types we discuss), but explicitly stop short of urging companies to shed the other two "value disciplines." Geoffrey Moore, with his

distinction of core versus context, in *Living on the Fault Line: Managing for Shareholder Value in the Age of the Internet* (New York: Harper Business, 2000), also promotes a form of specialization, urging executives to identify and focus simply on differentiating "activities." For a somewhat broader perspective on "deconstruction" that does not focus on the three distinctive business types, see Philip Evans and Thomas S. Wurster, *Blown to Bits: How the Economics of Information Transforms Strategy* (Boston: Harvard Business School Press, 2000); and Rudi K. Bresser, Michael A. Hitt, Robert D. Nixon, and Dieter Heuskel, *Winning Strategies in a Deconstructing World* (New York: John Wiley & Sons, 2000).

7. For this reason, we remain skeptical of the view of academics like Michael J. Piore and Charles F. Sabel, *The Second Industrial Divide* (New York: Basic Books, 1984); and Charles F. Sabel and Jonathan Zeitlin, "Historical Alternatives to Mass Production: Politics, Markets, and Technology in Nineteenth-Century Industrialization," *Past and Present* 108 (August 1985): 133–176, who anticipate that the mass-production paradigm of industrial organization will be replaced by a return to smaller, craft-based firms. The business landscape will certainly change in profound ways, but we do not expect smaller, craft-based firms to crowd out larger corporate entities.

8. Cliff Chen, partner, Crimson, interview with authors, January 19, 2004.

9. Prasad Ram, chief technology officer, Yahoo Software Development India, interview with authors, June 19, 2004.

10. Ibid.

11. Derek Holley, president, eTelecare, interview with authors, December 10, 2003.

12. An excellent overview of the ODM industry in Taiwan is provided by Salomon Smith Barney, "Silk Road to Silicon Road," equity research report, Salomon Smith Barney, March 22, 2002.

13. Salomon Smith Barney, "The ODM Model: Overview and Analysis," presentation in Palo Alto, CA, April 1, 2003.

14. Ibid.

15. John-Paul Ho, interview with authors, December 11, 2003.

16. Salomon Smith Barney, "Silk Road to Silicon Road."

17. An excellent overview of the digital still camera (DSC) industry in Taiwan is available in Morgan Stanley Dean Witter & Co., "Taiwan DSC Food Chain: Battle for the Sweet Spot," equity research report, Morgan Stanley Dean Witter & Co., July 4, 2003.

18. "David Ji and Ancle Hsu: Founders of Apex Digital," *Time*, December 2, 2002.

19. Drew Peck, "Leveraging Pacific Rim Capabilities to Build Global Companies," Crimson presentation, November 2003.

20. Mouli Raman, interview with authors, June 17, 2004.

21. "China's Telecom Forays Squeeze Struggling Rivals," *Wall Street Journal,* September 8, 2004, A1, A13.

22. C. K. Prahalad, *The Fortune at the Bottom of the Pyramid: Eradicating Poverty Through Profits* (Upper Saddle River, NJ: Wharton School Publishing, 2004), provides a broad range of examples of the product and process innovation stimulated by demanding emerging markets.

23. Rampraveen Swaminathan, vice president, Power Generation Business, Cummins India Ltd., e-mail to authors, September 5, 2004.

24. Nicholas Platt, "The Economic Ascendancy of China and India," speech to the Asia Society, Sydney, Australia, July 15, 2004.

Chapter 4

1. G. B. Richardson, "The Organization of Industry," *Economic Journal* 82 (September 1972): 883–896; and W. W. Powell, "Neither Market nor Hierarchy: Network Forms of Organization," *Research in Organizational Behavior* 12 (1990): 295–336, are viewed as key works in focusing attention on the role of business networks in economic activity. The topic of business networks has become more prominent in part because of growing interest in social network perspectives— for example, see James E. Rauch and Alessandra Casella, eds., *Networks and Markets* (New York: Russell Sage Foundation, 2001). Although many current discussions of business networks appear to view networks of cooperation among firms as a relatively new phenomenon, Fernand Braudel, *The Wheels of Commerce: Civilization and Capitalism, 15th–18th Century,* vol. 2 (New York: Harper and Row, 1979), reminds us that global commerce has been shaped by business networks over many centuries.

2. Since the mid-1990s, a rich literature has emerged on the topic of global production networks or commodity chains and has analyzed the disaggregation of the stages of production and their dispersion on a global scale. See especially Gary Gereffi and Miguel Korzeniewicz, eds., *Commodity Chains and Global Capitalism* (Westport, CT: Praeger, 1994); Timothy J. Sturgeon, "Turnkey Production Networks: A New American Model of Industrial Organization?" working paper 92A, Berkeley Roundtable on the International Economy, Berkeley, CA, 1997; Timothy J. Sturgeon, "How Do We Define Value Chains and Production Networks?" working paper 00–010, Massachusetts Institute of Technology Industrial Performance Center Globalization Study, Cambridge, MA, 2000; Michael Borrus, Dieter Ernst, and Stephan Haggard, eds., *International Production Networks in Asia: Rivalry or Riches?* (New York: Routledge, 2000); and Gary Gereffi, John Humphrey, and Timothy J. Sturgeon, "The Governance of Global Value Chains," *Review of International Political Economy,* forthcoming.

These works usually focus on the global organization of supply-chain management processes, while our perspective on process networks extends the concept to customer relationship management and product innovation and commercialization processes. Generally, these works remain at a relatively abstract level regarding the coordination mechanisms employed across these production networks, focusing on the structures of governance, rather than an analysis of the detailed practices of coordination. But for a detailed analysis of these coordination practices, see especially Gary Fields, *Territories of Profit: Communications, Capitalist Development and the Innovative Enterprises of G. F. Swift and Dell Computer* (Palo Alto, CA: Stanford University Press, 2004). For a provocative observation that buyer-driven global commodity chains are eventually becoming more prevalent over time than producer-driven commodity chains, see Gary Gereffi, "The Organization of Buyer-Driven Global Commodity Chains: How U.S. Retailers Shape Overseas Production Networks," in *Commodity Chains and Global Capitalism,* ed. Gary Gereffi and Miguel Korzeniewicz (Westport, CT: Praeger, 1994), 95–122. As a result of this high-level focus on governance structures, these works generally do not emphasize the notions of loose coupling or process orchestration across more than one level of a network—notions that we view as central to the functioning of process networks. For an interesting effort to quantify the extent of the disintegration of production and the growth of national economic specialization, see Robert Feenstra, "Integration of Trade and Disintegration of Production in the Global Economy," *Journal of Economic Perspectives* 12 (fall 1998): 31–50. Paul Duguid, "In Vino Veritas?" in *Locating Global Advantage: Industry Dynamics in the International Economy,* ed. Martin Kenney and Richard Florida (Palo Alto, CA: Stanford University Press, 2004); and Paul Duguid, "Brands and Supply Chains: Governance Before and After Chandler," in Contradictions et Dynamique des Organizations, ed. H. Dumez (Paris, Ecole Polytechnique: forthcoming), provide a badly needed historical perspective on the evolution of global supply chains and on the power relationships that shape this evolution.

    3. For more detail on Li & Fung, process networks, and process orchestration, see John Hagel, "Leveraged Growth: Expanding Sales Without Sacrificing Profits," *Harvard Business Review* (October 2002) pp. 68–77; and John Hagel, *Out of the Box: Strategies for Achieving Profits Today and Growth Tomorrow Through Web Services* (Boston: Harvard Business School Press, 2002), chap. 6. On Li & Fung more generally, see Joan Magretta, "Fast, Global and Entrepreneurial: Supply Chain Management, Hong Kong Style—An Interview with Victor Fung," *Harvard Business Review* (September–October 1998): 103–114; and Fred Young, "Li & Fung," Case 9-301-009 (Boston: Harvard Business School Press, 2000).

4. For a more detailed, and rigorous, discussion of economic webs, see John Hagel, "Spider Versus Spider," *McKinsey Quarterly* (1996); and John Hagel, *Net Worth: Shaping Markets When Customers Make the Rules* (Boston: Harvard Business School Press, 1999), chap. 6.

5. For more detail on orchestration, see Hagel, *Out of the Box*, chaps. 6 and 8; and John Hagel, John Seely Brown, and Scott Durchslag, "Orchestrating Loosely Coupled Business Processes: The Secret to Successful Collaboration," working paper, 2002, available at http://www.johnhagel.com/paper_orchestrating collaboration.pdf.

6. For a more detailed discussion of Nike's global process network, see James Brian Quinn, *Intelligent Enterprise: A Knowledge and Service Based Paradigm for Industry* (New York: Free Press, 1992).

7. There is an extensive literature on modularity in product design. Some of the most insightful works that begin to identify the implications of modularity in process and organization design are Richard N. Langlois and Paul L. Robertson, *Firms, Markets and Economic Change: A Dynamic Theory of Business Institutions* (London: Routledge, 1995); Carliss Y. Baldwin and Kim B. Clark, *Design Rules: The Power of Modularity* (Cambridge, MA: MIT Press, 2000); and Raghu Garud, Arun Kumaraswamy, and Richard N. Langlois, *Managing in the Modular Age: Architectures, Networks and Organizations* (Oxford: Blackwell, 2003). For a fascinating analysis of the role of modular product architectures in facilitating more "open" global production networks and the resulting impact on gaining competitive advantage relative to more "closed" production networks, see Michael Borrus, "The Resurgence of US Electronics: Asian Production Networks and the Rise of Wintelism," in *International Production Networks in Asia: Rivalry or Riches?* ed. Michael Borrus, Dieter Ernst, and Stephan Haggard (New York: Routledge, 2000), 57–79. Our concept of loose coupling and modularity in business processes differs from the concept of patching as developed in Shona L. Brown and Kathleen M. Eisenhardt, *Competing on the Edge: Strategy as Structured Chaos* (Boston: Harvard Business School Press, 1998). As described by Brown and Eisenhardt, patching focuses on modularity of businesses and products and mapping of the modules against market opportunities. Both concepts are inspired in part by the more general notion of patching as an adaptive search strategy, as described in Stuart Kauffman, *At Home in the Universe: The Search for the Laws of Self-Organization and Complexity* (New York: Oxford University Press, 1995).

8. The loose coupling of process networks may challenge some of the principles embodied in more tightly coupled "lean manufacturing" approaches like the Toyota production system, but the differences between these two approaches may be overstated. In this regard, see the suggestive characterization

offered in Stephen Spear and H. Kent Bowen, "Decoding the DNA of the Toyota Production System," *Harvard Business Review* (September–October 1999): 96–106: "the rules create an organization with a nested modular structure, rather like traditional Russian dolls that come one inside the other. The great benefit of nested, modular organizations is that people can implement design changes in one part without unduly affecting other parts." For a somewhat different but related view of loose coupling in organizations, see Karl E. Weick, "Organizational Culture as a Source of High Reliability," *California Management Review* 29 (winter 1987): 112–127; and Karl E. Weick, "Loosely Coupled Systems: A Reconceptualization," *Academy of Management Review* 15 (April 1990): 203–223.

9. For these reasons, we anticipate that loosely coupled process networks will become more prevalent across industries as product life cycles compress and as uncertainty increases. For an unduly neglected but rich treatment of the role of industry "clockspeeds" in shaping choices about the design of supply chains of capabilities, see Charles H. Fine, *Clockspeed: Winning Industry Control in the Age of Temporary Advantage* (Reading, MA: Perseus Books, 1998).

10. For more details on Cisco's process network, see John Hagel, *Out of the Box,* chap. 6.

11. While we are striking a more optimistic note here regarding the opportunity for companies in developed economies to use process networks to harness the specialized capabilities in offshore locations, we should note the perspective of Bruce Kogut, *Country Competitiveness: Technology and the Organization of Work* (New York: Oxford University Press, 1993), that organizing principles in business usually diffuse more rapidly among firms within a region than between regions and countries. Given that process networks are emerging most rapidly in Greater China, this may create a challenge for diffusion to the United States and Europe.

12. Much has been written about the evolving role of the multinational corporation as a mechanism to prospect for, leverage, and mobilize specialized capabilities on a global basis, but most of this literature remains very enterprise-centric, that is, concerned primarily with mechanisms within a single enterprise for leveraging distributed capabilities. See, for example, Yves Doz, Jose Santos, and Peter Williamson, *From Global to Metanational: How Companies Win in the Knowledge Economy* (Boston: Harvard Business School Press, 2001); Nitin Nohria and Sumantra Ghoshal, *The Differentiated Network: Organizing Multinational Corporations for Value Creation* (San Francisco: Jossey-Bass, 1997); and Sumantra Ghoshal and Christopher Bartlett, "The Multinational Corporation as an Interorganizational Network," *Academy of Management Review* 15 (1990): 603–625. Two books that place significant emphasis on the role of global production networks in accessing distributed specialized capability are Borrus,

Ernst, and Haggard, *International Production Networks in Asia;* and Martin Kenney and Richard Florida, eds., *Locating Global Advantage: Industry Dynamics in the International Economy* (Palo Alto, CA: Stanford University Press, 2004). For an interesting perspective on the relationship between specialized local business ecologies and more geographically dispersed networks of companies in the biotechnology industry, see Jason Owen-Smith and Walter W. Powell, "Knowledge Networks as Channels and Conduits: The Effects of Spillovers in the Boston Biotechnology Community," *Organization Science,* in press; and Kjersten Bunker Whittington, Jason Owen-Smith, and Walter W. Powell, "Spillovers Versus Embeddedness: The Contingent Effects of Propinquity and Social Structure," unpublished paper, Stanford University, Palo Alto, CA, July 2004. For a suggestive study on the concept of business networks as a set of distributed capabilities and issues associated with value creation and capture, see Bruce Kogut, "The Network as Knowledge: Generative Rules and the Emergence of Structure," *Strategic Management Journal* 21 (2000): 405–425. See also Gordon Walker, Bruce Kogut, and Weijian Shan, "Social Capital, Structural Holes and the Formation of an Industry Network," *Organization Science* 8 (1997): 109–112.

13. For a helpful view of the relationship between shared meaning and innovation, see Ilkka Tuomi, *Networks of Innovation: Change and Meaning in the Age of the Internet* (New York: Oxford University Press, 2002).

14. Tom Kelly, vice president of Internet Learning Solutions Group, Cisco Systems, interview with authors, June 6, 2003.

15. The importance of trust in specialization and collaboration throughout human history is highlighted in the provocative work by Paul Seabright, *The Company of Strangers: A Natural History of Economic Life* (Princeton, NJ: Princeton University Press, 2004). Seabright's distinction between calculation and reciprocity as twin foundations for trust helped shape our view that the opportunity for mutual capability building can be a particularly powerful motivator for building trust. For a provocative overview of the varying levels of social trust across national cultures and the implications for economic growth, see Francis Fukuyama, *Trust: The Social Virtues & The Creation of Prosperity* (New York: Free Press, 1995).

16. Our perspective on accelerating the building of trust differs from the concepts of "swift trust" or "active trust" developed by Debra Meyerson, Karl E. Weick, and Roderick M. Kramer, "Swift Trust and Temporary Groups," in *Trust in Organizations,* ed. Roderick M. Kramer and Tom R. Tyler (New York: Russell Sage Foundation, 1996): 166–195; and Anthony Giddens, *The Constitution of Society* (Cambridge, UK: Polity Press, 1984), in that both these concepts focus primarily on the challenge of rapidly building trust in temporary or transitional

situations. Our focus is how to rapidly build enduring trust among long-term business partners. Of course, there are parallels, including the central role of a contractor (i.e., an orchestrator) in helping to accelerate the building of trust.

17. For a useful overview of the role of trust in business relationships, see Christel Lane and Reinhard Bachmann, eds., *Trust Within and Between Organizations: Conceptual Issues and Empirical Applications* (New York: Oxford University Press, 1998). While many publications on trust in interfirm relationships focus on the importance of trust in reducing transaction costs, relatively few address the importance of trust in expanding the willingness and ability to share knowledge. In this context, see especially Mari Sako, "Does Trust Improve Business Performance?" in *Trust Within and Between Organizations: Conceptual Issues and Empirical Applications,* ed. Christel Lane and Reinhard Bachmann (New York: Oxford University Press, 1998); Charles F. Sabel, "Learning by Monitoring: The Institutions of Economic Development," in *Handbook of Economic Sociology,* ed. Neil Smelser and Richard Swedberg (Princeton, NJ: Princeton University Press, 1994); and Daniel Z. Levin and Rob Cross, "The Strength of Weak Ties You Can Trust: The Mediating Role of Trust in Effective Knowledge Transfer," *Management Science* 50 (November 2004): 1477–1490.

18. Victor Fung, group chairman, Li & Fung, Ltd., and William Fung, group managing director, Li & Fung, Ltd., interview with authors, August 11, 2002.

19. For a good summary of these classic problems, see Paul Milgrom and John Roberts, *Economics, Organization and Management* (Englewood Cliffs, NJ: Prentice Hall, 1992).

20. Fung and Fung, interview with authors.

21. For an overview of market-based reputation systems, see Daniel B. Klein, ed., *Reputation: Studies in the Voluntary Elicitation of Good Conduct* (Ann Arbor: University of Michigan Press, 1997). Peter Kollock, "The Production of Trust in Online Markets," *Advances in Group Processes* 16 (1999): 99–123, provides an interesting comparison of the relative merits of both negative and positive reputation systems. See also Chris Avery, Paul Resnick, and Richard Zeckhauser, "The Market for Evaluations," *American Economic Review* 89 (1999): 564–584, for a discussion of the viability of markets for evaluation systems, but note also the role that orchestrators in process networks can play as clearinghouses for reputation.

Chapter 5

1. Dorothy Leonard, *Wellsprings of Knowledge: Building and Sustaining the Sources of Innovation* (Boston: Harvard Business School Press, 1995). In Richard T. Pascale, *Managing on the Edge: How the Smartest Companies Use*

Conflict to Stay Ahead (New York: Simon and Schuster, 1990), the author high-lighted the importance of creative tension in high-performing companies, but his focus was much more at the level of broad, organizational design rather than on the creation of more targeted environments for innovative problem solving.

2. Our view of the importance of productive friction is shaped by a belief that tacit knowledge is growing in strategic importance as change accelerates and that both tacit knowledge and emergent practices are shaped in communities of practice that often have difficulty in engaging constructively with each other, both within and across enterprises. For further background on these beliefs and perspectives, see John Seely Brown and Paul Duguid, *The Social Life of Information* (Boston: Harvard Business School Press, 2000); Jean Lave and Etienne Wenger, *Situated Learning: Legitimate Peripheral Participation* (New York: Cambridge University Press, 1993); and Etienne Wenger, *Communities of Practice: Learning, Meaning and Identity* (New York: Cambridge University Press, 1998). Karin Knorr-Cetina's concept of epistemic cultures, as developed in her *Epistemic Cultures: How the Sciences Make Knowledge* (Cambridge, MA: Harvard University Press, 1999), helps us understand the challenges involved in sharing knowledge, especially across boundaries, both within and across firms. For a rich discussion of the relationships (and differences) between the concepts of communities of practice, networks of practice, and social capital, see Paul Duguid, "Incentivizing Practice," paper presented at ICTs and Social Capital in the Knowledge Society Workshop, Seville, November 2–3, 2003.

3. This distinction between enabling and coercive business processes is made in John Seely Brown and Paul Duguid, "Organizing Knowledge," *California Management Review* 40 (spring 1998): 90–111. See also the related concept of enabling and coercive bureaucracies in Paul Adler and Bryan Borys, "Two Types of Bureaucracy: Enabling and Coercive," *Administrative Science Quarterly* 41 (1996): 61–89. More generally, on the tension between practice and process within the enterprise, see John Seely Brown and Paul Duguid, "Creativity Versus Structure: A Useful Tension," *Sloan Management Review* (summer 2001): 93–94.

4. We are indebted to Tara Lemmey, founder and CEO, LENS Ventures, for the concept of action points.

5. See the classic work by Eric von Hippel, *The Sources of Innovation* (New York: Oxford University Press, 1988), regarding the role that lead users play in product innovation. More recently, C. K. Prahalad and Venkat Ramaswamy, *The Future of Competition: Co-Creating Unique Value with Customers* (Boston: Harvard Business School Press, 2004), have highlighted the growing importance of customers in "co-creating" products and services. Specifically on the collaborative role of a growing range of firms and other institutions in product innovation

processes, see Henry Chesbrough, *Open Innovation: The New Imperative for Creating and Profiting from Technology* (Boston: Harvard Business School Press, 2003).

6. Seely Brown and Duguid, "Organizing Knowledge."

7. The importance of respect from other participants and across communities of practice in productive friction is highlighted in John Seely Brown, foreword to *Organizations as Knowledge Systems,* ed. Haridimos Tsoukas and Nikos Mylonopoulos (Houndsmills, UK: Palgrave, 2003).

8. These practices are discussed in more detail in Steven Spear and H. Kent Bowen, "Decoding the DNA of the Toyota Production System," *Harvard Business Review* (September–October 1999): 96–106; and Jeffrey K. Liker, *The Toyota Way: Fourteen Management Principles from the World's Greatest Manufacturer* (New York: McGraw-Hill, 2004). See also Jeffrey H. Dyer and Kentaro Nobeoka, "Creating and Managing a High-Performance Knowledge-Sharing Network: The Toyota Case," *Strategic Management Journal* 21 (2000): 345–367, for an insightful discussion of the way Toyota structures and manages its production networks with suppliers to facilitate multidirectional knowledge flows across firm boundaries.

9. For more detailed discussions of the role of prototypes or boundary objects in enabling productive friction to occur, see Paul R. Carlile, "A Pragmatic View of Knowledge and Boundaries: Boundary Objects in New Product Development," *Organization Science* 13 (July–August 2002): 442–455; Paul R. Carlile, "Into the Black Box: The Knowledge Transformation Cycle," *Management Science* 49 (September 2003): 1180–1195; and Paul R. Carlile, "Transferring, Translating and Transforming: An Integrative Framework of Managing Knowledge Across Boundaries," unpublished paper, March 10, 2002 available at http://dspace.mit.edu/bitstream/1721.1/3959/2/EEL_3T.pdf. See also Susan Leigh Star and James R. Griesember, "Institutional Ecology, 'Translations' and Boundary Objects: Amateurs and Professionals in Berkeley's Museum of Vertebrate Zoology, 1907–1939," *Social Studies of Science* 19 (1989): 387–420; and Susan Leigh Star, "The Structure of Ill-Structured Solutions: Boundary Objects and Heterogeneous Distributed Problem Solving," in *Readings in Distributed Artificial Intelligence,* ed. M. Huhns and L. Glasser (Menlo Park, CA: Morgan Kaufman, 1989). For an interesting example of new forms of boundary objects enabled by technology, see Michael Schrage, *Serious Play: How the World's Best Companies Simulate to Innovate* (Boston: Harvard Business School Press, 2000).

10. Propagating practices within and across organizations is extremely challenging, even under the best of circumstances. For a discussion of these challenges, see especially the description of communities of practice and networks of practice in Seely Brown and Duguid, *The Social Life of Information.* See also

Paul Duguid, "'The Art of Knowing': Social and Tacit Dimensions of Knowledge and the Limits of the Community of Practice," *Information Society*, forthcoming.

11. Peter Beck, Mike Hildebrandt, Jeff Helmrick, and Betsy Delmonte, Beck Group, interviews with authors, July 2, 2004.

12. See especially Dongsheng Ge and Takahiro Fujimoto, "Quasi-Open Product Architecture and Technological Lock-In: An Exploratory Study on the Chinese Motorcycle Industry," *Annals of Business Administration Science* 3 (April 2004): 15–24; Dongsheng Ge, "The Architectural Attributes of Components and the Transaction Patterns of Detail Design Drawings: A Case Study on China's Motorcycle Industry," unpublished paper, International Motor Vehicle Program at MIT, Cambridge, MA, June 2003 (revision available at http://imvp .mit.edu/papers/0304/dongshengtakahiro.pdf); and Takahiro Fujimoto, Yasao Sugiyama, and Jun Otahara, "Chinese Motorcycle Industry: Why Product Architecture Matters," presentation at International Motor Vehicle Program at MIT Sponsor's Meeting, Cambridge, MA, September 19, 2002.

13. Dongsheng Ge, "Architectural Attributes of Components."

14. Thomas P. Murtha, Stefanie Ann Lenway, and Jeffrey A. Hart, *Managing New Industry Creation: Global Knowledge Formation and Entrepreneurship in High Technology* (Palo Alto, CA: Stanford University Press, 2001).

15. In addition to the works cited in note 2 above, on tacit knowledge, see especially Michael Polanyi, *The Tacit Dimension* (New York: Doubleday, 1966); and the related distinction between "know that" and "know how," developed by Gilbert Ryle, *The Concept of the Mind* (London: Hutchinson, 1949). See also a very suggestive treatment of the interplay between knowledge and information in Max H. Boisot, *Information Space: A Framework for Learning in Organizations, Institutions and Culture* (New York: Routledge, 1995).

16. The strategic importance of process network orchestrators will likely increase as this evolution from resource orchestration to innovation orchestration proceeds. For a provocative historical study highlighting the strategic value of creating a concentration point for knowledge flows, especially in rapidly changing and highly uncertain markets, see John F. Padgett and Christopher Ansell, "Robust Action and the Rise of the Medici, 1400–1434," *American Journal of Sociology* 98 (1993): 1259–1319.

17. By *shadow economy*, we refer to the vibrant, but unauthorized, economic exchanges that occur in most countries, but especially developing countries. Executives often view exception handling with some embarrassment and seek to downplay the extent of its operation. After all, companies invested a lot of effort and money in designing and implementing business processes that were supposed to handle all contingencies. Rather than viewing exception handling as

an embarrassment, executives must embrace this activity as an opportunity for innovation and capability building.

18. These are the obstacles that shape much of current thinking of the firm. For example, see Oliver E. Williamson's discussion of shirking, moral hazard, and opportunism, in *Markets and Hierarchies: Analysis and Antitrust Implications* (New York: Free Press, 1975); and Michael C. Jensen's exploration of principal-agent conflicts, in *A Theory of the Firm: Governance, Residual Claims and Organizational Forms* (Cambridge, MA: Harvard University Press, 2000). Paul Milgrom and John Roberts, *Economics, Organization and Management* (Englewood Cliffs, NJ: Prentice Hall, 1992), provide a useful view of the various coordination and incentive challenges shaping the formation and evolution of firms.

Chapter 6

1. For a relatively brief and accessible discussion of grid computing as one example of a virtualization architecture, see Ian Foster, "The Grid: Computing Without Bounds," *Scientific American* (April 2003): 79–85.

2. For a recent discussion of technology platforms addressing these issues, see Dan Farber, "Autonomous IT: Outsourcing Operations to Machines," *Release 1.0* (September 2004).

3. For more information on Charles Schwab and Google, see Lucas Mearian, "Schwab Goes Live with Grid Computing Technology," *Computerworld,* December 19, 2003; and Sanjay Ghemawat, Howard Gobioff, and Shun-Tak Leung, "The Google File System," working paper, University of Rochester, Rochester, NY, 2003, available at http://www.cs.rochester.edu/sosp2003/papers/p125-ghemawat.pdf.

4. For a relatively high-level view of service-oriented architectures, see Doug Kaye, *Loosely Coupled: The Missing Pieces of Web Services* (San Francisco: RDS Press, 2003), chap. 8.

5. For an introduction that focuses on the business impact of Web services technology, see John Hagel, *Out of the Box: Strategies for Achieving Profits Today and Growth Tomorrow Through Web Services* (Boston: Harvard Business School Press, 2002). For more technical discussions of Web services, see Kaye, *Loosely Coupled;* and Anne Thomas Manes, *Web Services: A Manager's Guide* (Boston: Addison-Wesley, 2003).

6. This is the essence of our critique of the perspective of Nicholas G. Carr, *Does IT Matter? Information Technology and the Corrosion of Competitive Advantage* (Boston: Harvard Business School Press, 2004). He argues that the commoditization of IT leads to diminishing potential for strategic advantage—

we would in fact assert the opposite. See John Hagel and John Seely Brown, "Even as a Commodity, IT Still Matters," *Financial Times,* January 18, 2004.

7. Martin Milani and John Seely Brown, "Security and Security Frameworks Within the Service Grids," in *Reflections on Web Services: A Compendium of Working Papers* (New York: Warburg Pincus, 2002), 1:80–96, also available as Martin Milani and John Seely Brown, "Some Security Considerations for Service Grids," working paper, http://www.johnhagel.com/paper_securitygrid.pdf. More broadly, three industry standards bodies are actively engaged in developing technology-based trust frameworks and standards for service-oriented architectures: the World Wide Web Consortium (W3C), the Organization for Advancement of Structured Information Standards (OASIS), and the Internet Engineering Task Force (IETF).

8. See, in particular, John Hagel and John Seely Brown, "Service Grids: The Missing Layer in Web Services," *Release 1.0* (December 2002); and John Hagel and John Seely Brown, "Service Grids: The Missing Link in Web Services," in *Reflections on Web Services: A Compendium of Working Papers* (Warburg Pincus, 2002), 1:37–54, also available at http://www.johnhagel.com/paper_servicegrid.pdf.

9. John Hagel, "Where Will Web Services Be Deployed?" parts 1 and 2 (June and July 2002), available at http://www.johnhagel.com/publications.html.

10. Tom Winans, John Seely Brown, and Nancy Martin, "A New Perspective on Web Services," in *Developing Mission Critical Service Oriented Architectures: A Compendium of Working Papers* (Warburg Pincus, 2003), 12–26, available at http://www.concentrum.com/papers/NewPerspectiveOnWebServices.pdf.

11. For good overviews of social software, see Esther Dyson, "Social Social Networks: Deodorant for the Soul?" *Release 1.0* (December 2003); Esther Dyson, "Social Networking for Business: Release 0.5," *Release 1.0* (November 2003); Jeff Ubois, "Online Reputation Systems," *Release 1.0* (October 2003); and Clay Shirky, "Social Software: A New Generation of Tools," *Release 1.0* (May 2003). See also Kara Swisher, " 'Wiki' May Alter How Employees Work Together," *Wall Street Journal,* July 29, 2004. A useful blog focusing on issues related to social software is available at http://www.corante.com/many.

12. John Seely Brown lived through this experience at Xerox and discussed some of its lessons in John Seely Brown and Paul Duguid, *The Social Life of Information* (Boston: Harvard Business School Press, 2000). See also Daniel G. Bobrow and Jack Whalen, "Community Knowledge Sharing in Practice: The Eureka Story," *Reflections: The SoL Journal* 4 (winter 2002): 47–59; Yutaka Yamauchi, Jack Whalen, and Daniel G. Bobrow, "Information Use of Service Technicians in Difficult Cases," paper presented at the INTERACT 2003 Conference on Human-Computer Interaction, Zurich, Switzerland, September 2003; and Julian

Orr, *Talking About Machines: An Ethnography of a Modern Job* (New York: IRL Press, 1996).

13. Rick Davis, CEO, DAVACO Sourcing, interview with authors, August 2, 2004.

14. Tom Kelly, vice president of Internet Learning Solutions Group, Cisco Systems, interviews with authors, June 6, 2003. See also Patricia A. Galagan, "Delta Force," *Training and Development* (July 2002): 20–22; Patricia A. Galagan, "Mission E-Possible: The Cisco E-Learning Story," *Training and Development* (February 2001): 2–8; "Cisco's Quick Study," *Fast Company,* October 2000.

15. "The ABC's of VoIP," *Business Week,* September 21, 2004; and Stephanie Mehta, "The Future Is on the Line," *Fortune,* July 12, 2004.

16. See, for example, Cisco Cheng, "Viditel," *PC Magazine,* December 9, 2003.

17. The impact that these new architectures and tools will have on business practices and organizations will be far-reaching. For a rich view of the interplay between technology and business organization, see Wanda J. Orlikowski, "Using Technology and Constituting Structures: A Practice Lens for Studying Technology in Organizations," *Organization Science* 11 (July–August 2000): 404–428. Also, it is important to recognize the significant lead times that often separate technology innovation from broader changes in the business landscape, as Carlota Perez forcefully reminds us, in *Technological Revolutions and Financial Capital: The Dynamics of Bubbles and Golden Ages* (Northampton, MA: Edward Elgar, 2002).

Chapter 7

1. A useful overview of the evolution of schools of business strategy since the mid-1950s can be found in Henry Mintzberg, Bruce Ahlstrand, and Joseph Lampel, *Strategy Safari: A Guided Tour Through the Wilds of Strategic Management* (New York: Free Press, 1998).

2. For classic statements of this planning school of strategy, see H. Igor Ansoff, *Corporate Strategy* (New York: McGraw Hill, 1965); and George Steiner, *Top Management Planning* (New York: MacMillan, 1969). Early views of strategy as positioning can be found in Bruce D. Henderson, *Henderson on Corporate Strategy* (Cambridge, MA: Abt Books, 1979); and Michael E. Porter, *Competitive Advantage: Creating and Sustaining Superior Performance* (New York: Free Press: 1985).

3. Perhaps one of the most well-known statements of this perspective is Amar V. Bhide, "Hustle as Strategy," *Harvard Business Review* 64 (September–October 1986): 59–65.

4. For a strong discussion of strategy under uncertainty, see Hugh Courtney, *Twenty/Twenty Foresight: Crafting Strategy in an Uncertain World* (Boston:

Harvard Business School Press, 2001). Real options theory is one of the disciplines used to support strategies of movement—see especially Avinash K. Dixit and Robert S. Pindyck, *Investment Under Uncertainty* (Princeton, NJ: Princeton University Press, 1994); and Tom Copeland and Vladimir Antikarov, *Real Options: A Practitioner's Guide* (New York: Texere, 2001). Another discipline that has helped shape strategies of movement is business dynamics—see John D. Sterman, *Business Dynamics: Systems Thinking and Modeling for a Complex World* (Boston: McGraw-Hill, 2000). Finally, game theory has also contributed to strategies of movement—see Avinash K. Dixit and Barry J. Nalebuff, *Thinking Strategically: The Competitive Edge in Business, Politics, and Everyday Life* (New York: W. W. Norton, 1991). Of course, these disciplines are broadly valuable and do not demand adherence to extreme forms of strategies of movement.

5. Eric Beinhocker, *The Origin of Wealth* (Boston: Harvard Business School Press, in press), offers the most eloquent application of complexity theory to the field of business strategy.

6. "What Doth It Profit?" *Economist,* December 6, 2001, 65; "A Survey of the World Economy," *Economist,* September 28, 2002, 9; and Richard Foster and Sarah Kaplan, *Creative Destruction: Why Companies That Are Built to Last Underperform the Market—and How to Successfully Transform Them* (New York: Currency Doubleday, 2001), 12–13.

7. Disruptive innovations rarely emerge in core business arenas. Instead, they take root on the edge and gather momentum before targeting the core, so a longer-term view of the business forces executives to explore the edges to identify potential disruptions. The tendency for disruptive innovations to emerge on the edge of network infrastructures like railroads, telegraphs, and telephones is documented by Harmeet Sawhney in "The Public Telephone Network: Stages in Infrastructure Development," *Telecommunications Policy* 16 (September–October 1992): 538–552 and "Wi-Fi Networks and the Rerun of the Cycle," *Info* (5): 25–33.

8. There are many accounts of the early history of Microsoft, but see especially Randall E. Stross, *The Microsoft Way: The Real Story of How the Company Outsmarts Its Competition* (Reading, MA: Addison-Wesley, 1996).

9. Some tools that can assist senior management teams in framing common perspectives around long-term direction include scenario planning—see especially Peter Schwartz, *The Art of the Long View* (New York: Doubleday Currency, 1991); and Kees Van der Heijden, *Scenarios: The Art of Strategic Conversation* (New York: John Wiley, 1996)—and related structured processes for challenging senior executives to question and reshape their mental models, as discussed in Foster and Kaplan, *Creative Destruction*.

10. Gary Hamel and C. K. Prahalad, *Competing for the Future: Breakthrough*

Strategies for Seizing Control of Your Industry and Creating the Markets of Tomorrow (Boston: Harvard Business School Press, 1994).

11. However, Hamel and Prahalad's use of strategic intent was much broader and less targeted than the concept of long-term direction that we are describing. For example, their first illustration of strategic intent in *Competing for the Future* was the statement by British Airways that it aspired to become "The World's Favourite Airline." This aspiration might implicitly contain answers to the three questions we identify as a test for an effective long-term direction, but as presented, it appears much too general to force the difficult choices executives will confront.

12. For two perspectives on shaping strategies, see John Hagel and Marc Singer, *Net Worth: Shaping Markets When Customers Make the Rules* (Boston: Harvard Business School Press, 1999), chap. 6; and Courtney, *Twenty/Twenty Foresight,* chap. 3.

13. For examples of recent perspectives on strategy as a form of experimentation, see Eric D. Beinhocker, "Robust Adaptive Strategies," in *Strategic Thinking for the Next Economy,* ed. Michael A. Cusumano and Constantinos C. Markides (San Francisco: Jossey-Bass, 2001); and Lowell L. Bryan, "Just-in-Time Strategies for a Turbulent World," *McKinsey Quarterly* (2002 special ed., *Risk and Resilience*): 16–27.

14. Michael L. Tushman and Charles A. O'Reilly, *Winning Through Innovation: A Practical Guide to Leading Organizational Change and Renewal* (Boston: Harvard Business School Press, 1997). The FAST approach, by creating productive friction through the simultaneous management of long-term and short-term horizons, may help senior management overcome the "innovator's dilemma," as framed in Clayton M. Christensen, *The Innovator's Dilemma: When New Technologies Cause Great Firms to Fail* (Boston: Harvard Business School Press, 1997); and Clayton M. Christensen and Michael E. Raynor, *The Innovator's Solution: Creating and Sustaining Successful Growth* (Boston: Harvard Business School Press, 2003).

15. This distinction between single-loop and double-loop learning was suggested by Chris Argyris and Donald Schon, *Organizational Learning: A Theory of Action Perspective* (Reading, MA: Addison-Wesley, 1978).

16. For classic statements of the challenges of organizational inertia, see Michael T. Hannan and John Freeman, "The Population Ecology of Organizations," *American Journal of Sociology* 82 (1977): 929–964; and Michael T. Hannan and John Freeman, "Structural Inertia and Organizational Change," *American Sociological Review* 49 (1984): 149–164. For a discussion of the distinction between radical incrementalism and incremental radicalism, see John Seely Brown, "Seeing Differently: A Role for Pioneering Research," *Research Technology Management* 41 (May–June 1998): 24–33.

17. A psychologist, Kenneth Craik, first developed the concept of mental models in 1943 to describe the mind-sets that shape our actions. This concept of mental models is more fully described in Philip N. Johnson-Laird, *Mental Models* (Cambridge, MA: Harvard University Press, 1983).

18. As Ronald S. Burt, *Structural Holes: The Social Structure of Competition* (Cambridge: Harvard University Press, 1992), reminds us, holes in the social structure of competitive arenas create opportunities for high rates of return, and differential access to these holes can become a source of strategic advantage.

Index

About the Authors

John Hagel III is a management consultant, public speaker, and author based in Silicon Valley. As a consultant, he works with senior management to shape business strategies and improve business performance. His experience includes senior management positions in technology businesses and sixteen years with McKinsey & Company, where he served as a leader of its Strategy Practice and founder and leader of its Electronic Commerce Practice.

As an author, John has written numerous books, including his most recent one, *Out of the Box: Strategies for Achieving Profits Today and Growth Tomorrow through Web Services*, and the business-book bestsellers, *Net Gain: Expanding Markets through Virtual Communities* (coauthored with Arthur Armstrong) and *Net Worth: Shaping Markets When Customers Make the Rules* (coauthored with Marc Singer). He has written widely in the business press, including six articles in *Harvard Business Review*, two of which won McKinsey Awards for best articles of the year (including one coauthored with John Seely Brown).

For more information about John and his most recent perspectives, visit his Web site, www.johnhagel.com. His e-mail address is john@johnhagel.com.

John Seely Brown is the former Chief Scientist of Xerox Corporation and former director of its Palo Alto Research Center (PARC). He is currently a visiting scholar at the University of Southern California in the areas of digital media and digital culture. He has written widely on the management of innovation, organizational learning, social systems, and the roles of IT in enabling new kinds of business strategies.

He has published over one hundred papers and four books. His book *The Social Life of Information*, coauthored with Paul Duguid, has been translated into nine languages. He has written three articles for *Harvard Business Review* and won two McKinsey Awards for the best article of the year (one with John Hagel III).

He is a frequent public speaker, serves on the board of directors of several public and private companies, and is a trustee of Brown University and the John D. and Catherine T. MacArthur Foundation.

John has received numerous honors and awards including honorary degrees from Brown University, the London School of Business, and Claremont Graduate University.

For more information about John, visit his Web site, www.johnseelybrown.com.